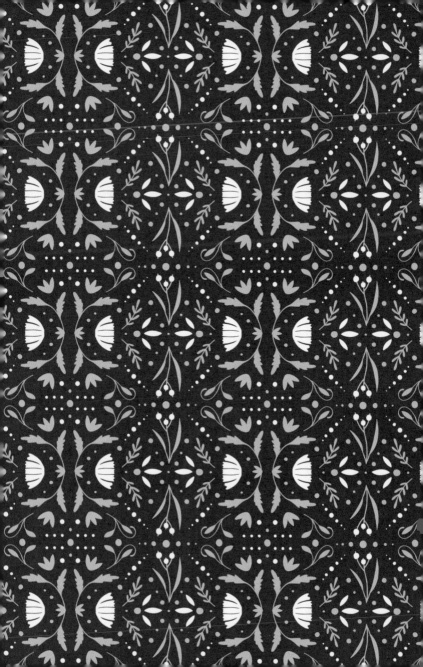

TO

_____

FROM

_____

DATE

_____

IN THIS

TOGETHER

90 DEVOTIONS ON THE
Book of Ephesians

DaySpring

LIVE YOUR FAITH

In This Together: 90 Devotions on the Book of Ephesians
Copyright © 2023 DaySpring Cards, Inc. All rights reserved.
First Edition, September 2023

Published by:

DaySpring

21154 Highway 16 East
Siloam Springs, AR 72761
dayspring.com

Written by: Bonnie Rickner Jensen
Cover Design by: Hannah Brinson

Printed in China
Prime: J9590
ISBN: 978-1-64870-915-9

CONTENTS

INTRODUCTION

*W*e are all parts of one body, we have the same Spirit, and we have all been called to the same glorious future" (Ephesians 4:4 TLB). These are the true and powerful words of Paul, while imprisoned, to the people of Ephesus. This book is a celebratory message of God's welcome into the riches of heaven, extended to *all* of us—not some of us. In Jesus we become one, and we're in the throes of this life together. By way of His sacrifice, He united us and became a perfect example of how we should love one another. *"Be humble and gentle. Be patient with each other, making allowance for each other's faults because of your love. Try always to be led along together by the Holy Spirit and so be at peace with one another"* (Ephesians 4:2-3 TLB)

This devotional walk through the book of Ephesians will take you by the hand and lead you by God's heart to the place of knowing that togetherness has *always* been part of His plan. We're on a journey of learning to love like Christ and understand the importance of unity. Walking together is necessary to our light in this dark, searching world.

A POWERFUL UNION

*I pray that you will begin to understand
how incredibly great His power is to help those
who believe Him. It is that same mighty power
that raised Christ from the dead and seated Him
in the place of honor at God's right hand.*

EPHESIANS 1:19–20 TLB

How do we navigate our way out of a period of time when separation feels safe and togetherness feels like a test of our faith? We move forward knowing every trial comes to an end and every test strengthens and stretches our trust in God. Darkness is dispelled by the brightness of a love that can't be dimmed. God's love is our compass through every storm. Even when it feels impossible to believe, purpose emerges from suffering and sorrow.

God's unfailing purpose reigns supreme through every period of time (see Ephesians 1:10). The goodness of God can't be submerged, no matter how devastating our difficulties. The depth of our pain creates a powerful pull toward the source of our courage, resolve, and restoration. God is with us. He is our Captain, our Companion, and our Comforter. His prevailing purpose is setting our course. The togetherness we need most is our union with Christ. That's where the power lies—and it lives in you.

I pray for Your power to be revealed
in everything I face today, Lord.
Nothing is greater than the strength in me
when I depend on You.

AN ESSENTIAL EXCHANGE

Praise God. . .who has blessed us
with every blessing in heaven
because we belong to Christ.

EPHESIANS 1:3 TLB

There's no "go-it-alone" message woven through the Word of God. Our lives depend on being joined with Christ in complete surrender. Every spiritual blessing, and in turn every earthly blessing, comes to us through Him. We need Jesus, and Jesus taught us to need each other. Being in perfect oneness with God, He could've walked His earthly journey alone, but He chose not to. His example is our lead. We are here for each other. We're better when we're surrounded by those who encourage us and by those who look to us for encouragement. It opens the door to a continual exchange of love and comfort, two essential gifts for our survival in life.

This world is often dark and difficult. The people God brings into our lives can offer light, direction, and purpose. Keeping our hearts open and our spirits sensitive will guide us into the fullest measure of love God intends for us to have in this one, priceless life He's given.

I pray my life reflects the welcome,
loving heart You desire me to have, Lord.
Help me see the needs in front of me
with the eyes of Jesus.

PULLING US BACK TOGETHER

He chose us in Him before the foundation
of the world, that we should be holy
and without blame before Him in love.

❥· EPHESIANS 1:4 NKJV ·❦

We might never be chosen first for anything in our lives—the team, the promotion, the partner, the position. Yet before creating the world in which we live, God chose you. He saw you through the lens of the love He sent to save us. You were first on His mind, the reason the story of redemption was written. What an astounding truth it is to know the value God places on a life. Every person we know, everyone we pass on the street, every face we see walking through the grocery store. . .God deemed worth the sacrifice of His Son. That's why it's invaluable to live a life that reminds others they're chosen, they're priceless, and that God thought of them first—long before the world around them made them feel otherwise.

We have a thousand seemingly small and insignificant opportunities every day to be an expression of God's love. Each one is vitally important. It can lift someone closer to the One who holds them in a place of infinite value. The darkness in this world strives to push us away from each other, but love has the power to pull us back together.

Let me be one who sees and seizes
every chance to love someone,
Lord. Show me ways to remind others
they're priceless to You.

LIVING PROOF

*He has showered down upon us
the richness of His grace—
for how well He understands us
and knows what is best for us at all times.*

EPHESIANS 1:8 TLB

Being known is one of the most beautiful reflections of love. We're seen and understood perfectly by God because His love for us is flawless. Knowing what is best for us includes knowing who is best for us. We have friends who challenge us and those who comfort us, some we've known a lifetime and others a short time. Yet we should never become so comfortable in our relationships that we miss God's constant movement in our lives. People are His passion, and we're called to be living proof of His love. Meeting new people can inspire us to prayerfully ask the questions, "What does this person need from me that will help them see You?" or "What do I need to see in this person that will help me be more like You?"

God's best will always be centered around the

relationships in our lives. He created us for them. Life is hard, and love is needed more than ever. When we look for ways to show love, we open our hearts to receive it. Where love is, God is—in the most fulfilling, life-changing, world-shaking way.

I want to be Your love language on this earth, Lord. Deepen my desire to express it wherever I go, with everyone I meet.

STRONGER
TOGETHER

He thought of everything,
provided for everything we could possibly need,
letting us in on the plans He took
such delight in making.

EPHESIANS 1:9 The Message

At some point in our lives, we realize our relationships are everything. Possessions are temporal, feelings are fleeting, and time is racing. God, in providing everything we could possibly need, chose us for one another—to lean on and love; to confide in and laugh with; to encourage, embrace, and enjoy. Relationships are a thing we need and something God takes delight in giving.

Sometimes on our darkest days and in our most difficult trials, we have a tendency to isolate ourselves and endure our battles alone. We trust God is with us, but we don't want to burden anyone else with our pain and suffering. We justify this by telling ourselves that everyone is walking through tough stuff, so they don't need one more thing to think about. This is a temptation designed to keep us separated from God's plan for our lives. His plan always includes the people He brings into our lives, the relationships He orchestrates, and the purpose they hold in being a part of our journey of faith. We are stronger together, braver side by side, and perseveringly hopeful hand in hand—every step of the way to our eternal home.

In my difficult times, teach me to be open
to the love and compassion of others, Lord.
Thank You for bringing them into my life.

CONNECTIONS

It's in Christ that we find out who we are
and what we are living for.

> EPHESIANS 1:11 THE MESSAGE

It's impossible to realize the abundant, purposeful life we're created for without finding out who we are in Christ. He's the revelation of our true self, the illumination of our divine purpose, and the only hope we have of fulfilling every good thing we desire to do. Being present when we were created and having bridged our sin-broken relationship with God, Jesus knows the breadth of our lives from beginning to end. He knew the scope of our earthly potential the moment we were born. Our lives are lived as fully as they should be when we're fully surrendered to Him.

As the saying goes, "That's what Jesus does. He loves us and He knows things." In truth, He knows everything—and that's a good thing. As our constant companion, He's an infallible guide for our hearts on how to build and nurture relationships, how to stay mindful of loving people like God does, and how to discern the unspoken needs around us. Every step of His earthly walk was in step with God's will because He understood that what He was living for was the people God put in His path on purpose. Our deepest desire should be to love people—being confident our connections are a part of God's plan.

*Fill me with the desire to love others
like You do, Lord.*

PERFECT ORDER

Ever since I first heard
of your strong faith in the Lord Jesus
and your love for God's people everywhere,
I have not stopped thanking God for you.

EPHESIANS 1:15–16 NLT

Paul's heart was overwhelmed with gratefulness for the people who loved God and were in turn loving God's people everywhere. That's the perfect order for our lives. Love God, love people. It doesn't matter where they live or where they worship. It doesn't matter if we see eye to eye on worldly issues or how far apart we are on them. Love God, love people. It's as simple as that, and sometimes, just as difficult. Every moment we spend defining or magnifying our differences is a moment stolen from love's life-changing power.

Love leads. It leads people to believe in their infinite worth. It leads people to believe there is still light and hope in the darkness. It leads people to believe there is compassion, kindness, and goodness to be found—and it leads their hearts to the Source of them all. Love

God, love people. Let it be our first thought when we start our day and the thing we're remembered for when we've taken our last breath. Love is the only way to make an eternal difference in a temporal world—and we can make the biggest impact together.

*I pray my heart is an overflowing vessel
of love for You and everyone in my life, Lord.*

ACT FIRST

God is so rich in mercy. . .
He gave us back our lives again
when He raised Christ from the dead—
only by His undeserved favor
have we ever been saved.

 **EPHESIANS 2:4–5 TLB**

It's hard to comprehend that we're richer than we can imagine and favored beyond measure without having done a single thing to earn it. Love acted first and asked for nothing. There are no conditions set forth or standards to meet to qualify for God's love and mercy. We don't deserve it, but we don't have the power to stop it. The love we show each other should look like the love God showed us—act first, and ask for nothing.

We're living in a time when giving the things that hold eternal value matters more than ever. We need to be proactive about love and forgiveness, compassion and kindness, tenderness and empathy. As our lives feel like they're speeding up through advances in technology, the pressures of work schedules, and the general hurriedness of day-to-day routines, taking time to invest in our relationships is slowing to a standstill. It's important to look around and see where love can act mercifully—when friends need a visit, not a text; when our families need our presence; when a stranger needs a smile. God will bring the opportunities—it's up to us to bring the action.

*Align my hands and feet with Your heart, Lord,
to put love in action every day.*

LIVING EXAMPLES

*God can always point to us
as examples of how very, very rich His kindness is,
as shown in all He has done for us
through Jesus Christ.*

➤• EPHESIANS 2:7 TLB •◀

What if we lived every day with a constant awareness that we're examples of God's kindness? A kindness that looks outwardly and behaves selflessly. A kindness that leaves everyone in our wake with the feeling they're seen, valued, and loved. Eyes are searching, hearts are aching, and God is moving to change lives through us. If we become living examples of God's love, we exercise our superpower in this difficult, ever-changing world. The key to unleashing it is being there for one another, reaching out to meet the needs of others, and cultivating love and kindness in our homes.

God has shown immeasurable kindness to us through all He's done. Maybe it's time to be doers? It's easy to get caught up in the web of our own lives, spending all our energy taking care of what's in front of us. When we do, we lose sight of His command to "share each other's troubles and problems" (Galatians 6:2 TLB). Our most fulfilling life comes by fulfilling the desires of God's heart. He created us for togetherness, and together we are stronger, more kind, more loved, and more alive.

There will be chances to be a kind example today, Lord.
Lead me to be a reflection of You.

GENEROUSLY GOOD

Saving is all His idea, and all His work.
All we do is trust Him enough to let Him do it.
It's God's gift from start to finish!

EPHESIANS 2:8-9 The Message

Being generous with our time and resources isn't always easy, but it's always good. Our time here is a journey of learning to love God deeply, serve Him sacrificially, and glorify Him gratefully—for the eternal gift He's given us so graciously. When a friend, neighbor, family member, or even a stranger is in need, we sometimes hesitate to be a blessing because we have so much going on personally. We're tempted to decline helping because we're strained mentally and physically, believing we have nothing left to give or enough time to spend. But if we trust God to direct our steps and sustain our strength, every need before us is a chance to glorify Him through what we do.

We have the privilege of showing this world every day what God is like. If the things we do mirror the things He is—love, kindness, and compassion—we magnify His goodness and gain eternal ground. This is how God brings us together right here, right now. . . while turning our hearts to the hope of eternity.

I never want to turn a blind eye
or neglect a chance to be generous
with my time and resources, Lord.
Give me a greater desire
to serve You wholeheartedly.

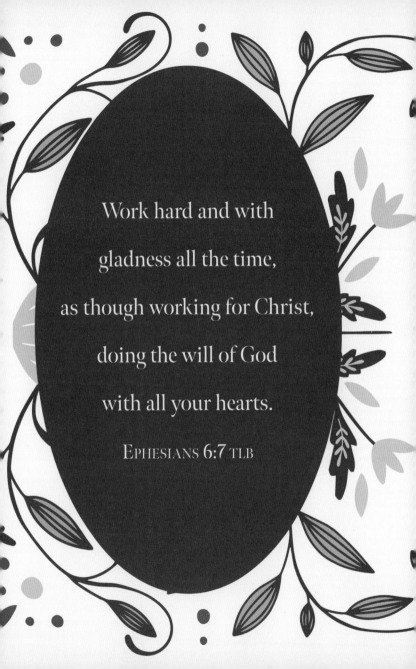

Work hard and with
gladness all the time,
as though working for Christ,
doing the will of God
with all your hearts.

EPHESIANS 6:7 TLB

OUR HAPPIEST MOMENTS

We are His workmanship,
created in Christ Jesus for good works.

▶ EPHESIANS 2:10 NKJV ◀

We weren't created to go through life grinding away our years reaching goals while spending our leftover time reaching out. We need each other, and we need to remind each other on a daily basis how incredibly good God has been to bring us together. The relationships we have are His way of loving us in a very personal way. When we let the rush of life push us apart, we miss out on the fullness of joy God wants us to have.

C.S. Lewis wrote, "As long as we have the itch of self-regard we shall want the pleasure of self-approval; but the happiest of moments are those when we forget our precious selves and have neither, but have everything else (God, our fellow humans, animals, the garden, and the sky) instead." We were created for good works—the things that have love woven into them and the ways that show the people in our lives how much God cares for them and how present He is. God gets the praise when our priorities are in place—and investing in our fellow humans will always lead to our happiest moments.

Use me for good works today, Lord.
I'm thankful to be Your workmanship.

CHOOSE TO EXUDE

I pray that the eyes of your heart
may be enlightened in order that you may know
the hope to which He has called you.

EPHESIANS 1:18 NIV

HOPE. It's powerful and contagious. We should pray every morning for God to open wide the eyes of our heart to ignite the hope inside us. He has called us to this life-changing force because He knows what it can do in a world losing sight of it. A single thirty-minute newscast can dim the light of the hope we've been given if we're not careful. In direct contrast, we can choose to exude the hope of our calling and spread it to every person in our lives and everyone we encounter throughout our day. What we have isn't a fleeting hope that fades or falters; it's the eternal hope that was achieved at the empty tomb. It cannot fail. "We have this hope as an anchor for the soul, firm and secure" (Hebrews 6:19 NIV).

"Hope does not disappoint, because the love of God has been poured out in our hearts" (Romans 5:5 NKJV).

We have hope because we're loved with an infinite, infallible love. God wants us to live the love that leads to the hope incapable of letting us down. Let's light the world with it today.

We're called to encourage one another
with the hope You give, Lord.
Open the eyes of my heart today
to see who needs Your love.

BEING A
REMINDER

Christ Himself is our way of peace.

❧ EPHESIANS 2:14 TLB ❧

It's good to be alone when we're in prayer, when we need to hear the still, small voice of God as we seek answers and direction. Equally good and as essential to living the life God created us to live is being together—physically present for one another—to offer encouragement, comfort, and strength. It's true for the elderly living alone in our neighborhoods. It's true for the neglected child, the recently widowed family member, and the single or divorced friend. Jesus is our constant comfort, and we are now His hands, His feet, and His love to those around us. "In response to all He has done for us, let us outdo each other in being helpful and kind to each other and in doing good" (Hebrews 10:24 TLB).

Good things driven by love and done for the glory of God are the only things that will last beyond the lives we're living. A kindness shown, an encouraging word

spoken, a helping hand offered, a simple hug given—
each one becomes a reminder that we're not alone in
this difficult world. Knowing we're not alone gives us
peace of heart and mind, which God has given in fullest
measure through Jesus, who is our way of peace.

Let me be a reminder to someone every day
of Your peace and presence, Lord.

A BEAUTIFUL WHOLE

We who believe are carefully joined together with Christ as parts of a beautiful, constantly growing temple for God.

EPHESIANS 2:21 TLB

There are no accidents or coincidental connections in our lives. We are carefully joined together with Jesus, and every relationship we have is part of His plan for our lives. We are intricate pieces of a beautiful whole. God was intentional about creating us for each other. Nothing is out of place when it comes to the way our lives are intertwined and put together. Our people are ours on purpose. Putting our focus on them is central to our well-being. Then together, keeping our hearts open to others by being expressions of love, care, generosity, and compassion, we honor God and change the world.

We might not be chosen to reach the masses through books or on stages, but life by life, day after day, we amass the eternal impact for which we're designed.

Each of us is a unique and vital life with a necessary and irreplaceable role to play in the lives of others. Today is going to bring new chances to fulfill God's will for our lives—and we can be sure they will affect someone else's.

I believe You created me to be an important part of Your perfect plan, Lord. Keep my eyes focused on You.

A LASTING IMPRESSION

When we trust in Him,
we're free to say whatever needs to be said,
bold to go wherever we need to go.

EPHESIANS 3:12 THE MESSAGE

There are times when God prompts us to say or do something for someone and we hesitate to follow through for fear of rejection or a negative response. Overcoming the hesitation is a process of learning to trust God completely. Reactions are not our responsibility, but obedience is. When God is asking us to act, the "nudging" won't let up. We're on this earth to carry each other along, to walk side by side, to encourage hope, and to do it with a spirit of humility and joy.

If we're not careful and prayerful, we can fall into a habit of thinking what we do is more important than who we are. Just as our presence is often more of a blessing than the physical projects we do, our kind, loving, and positive attitude can leave the most meaningful impression. The eternal work of our amazing God in the hearts of humans is unseen, but His presence is what we hope people perceive in us. It's what they'll remember. It's what they'll think about when our good deeds are finished. The love that inspires us is the thing that will last—even when the things we do are long past.

Give me courage to follow Your prompts, Lord.
Make me confident in the steps
I take to reflect Your love.

LOOKING OUTWARD

Now to Him who is able to do exceedingly
abundantly above all that we ask or think,
according to the power that works in us,
to Him be glory.

EPHESIANS 3:20–21 NKJV

What would we ask God to do through us, being confident that His life-giving power is actively working in our lives? The thing we should want exceedingly, abundantly above all else is to make a difference in the lives of others. Eternal blessings infinitely outweigh material ones, and there's nothing more fulfilling than turning our attention from ourselves to another person. Looking outward keeps us leaning on our Source of strength and provision. Being a continuous channel of love pouring into the lives of others is the surest way to experience every heavenly blessing we've been given in Christ. While in this world, He became our example of being constantly aware of the needs around us.

Going through life with tunnel vision and blinders on is the surest way to miss the greatest blessings God puts in our path. His most beautiful gifts come to us to flow through us. The more we give, the more we're given. "What happens when we live God's way? He brings gifts into our lives, much the same way that fruit appears in an orchard—things like affection for others, exuberance about life, serenity" (Galatians 5:22 THE MESSAGE).

Make my life a wealth of love for people, Lord.
Let me always be a useful, willing vessel.

FORMING A
LIFELINE

I ask Him to strengthen you by His spirit—
not a brute strength but a glorious inner strength—
that Christ will live in you as you open the door
and invite Him in.

EPHESIANS 3:14 THE MESSAGE

A glorious inner strength. We pray we have it today. We tap in to it for the encouragement of others, every day. It comes to us by throwing the door of our hearts open to the presence and power of Jesus. We can get spiritually lazy and take for granted the fact that He never leaves us, not even for a moment. We can follow routines, trudge through our days, check off our to-do lists, and plan our time in calendar-reminder increments—all the while neglecting to pause and ask for God's input. His instruction will likely include something we can do for someone else to reflect the love we depend on. It might be showing more patience, being more present, or extending a seemingly unnoticeable kindness.

Everything we do in love's service makes a significant difference in this world, and God sees it. God loves it. Over time these differences add up. They form a lifeline from the heavenly realm to our earthly home and into people's lives. When schedules are gone and calendars cease to exist, what we have done motivated by God's love lasts—hopefully having an eternal effect.

Help me to slow down and look around today, Lord.
My heart is open to You.

MORE AND MORE

I pray that Christ
will be more and more at home
in your hearts, living within you
as you trust in Him.

EPHESIANS 3:17 TLB

How is it that we feel comfortable and at home in a place to which we're invited? Maybe we're met with excitement and open arms when we arrive. Maybe the surroundings are peaceful and quiet. Maybe we feel welcomed by the love we're given while we're there. Paul prayed that Christ would be more and more at home in our hearts—and how can that be? One of the most important ways is by the attention we give to Him in our daily lives. "In everything you do, put God first, and He will direct you and crown your efforts with success" (Proverbs 3:6 TLB).

The more time we spend with the One who abides in our hearts, the more love we'll feel, the more joy we'll experience, and the more peace we'll have. When we acknowledge His presence in everything we do, we bring His love to everyone we're around. There will be a peace in us that draws people to relax, hope, and rest—a quiet assurance that God is here, and that we are here for others too.

Be at home in my heart today, Lord.
Saturate my being with Your presence
and direct me with Your perfect love.

EQUALLY IMPORTANT

May your roots go down deep
into the soil of God's marvelous love.

➤• EPHESIANS 3:17 TLB •◄

The deepest desire of every person in this world is to be loved—loved as they are and wherever they are on their life journeys. God has eternally satisfied that desire through Jesus. We have a lifelong calling to extend His love to every person we meet. The dark, difficult days we all face can tempt us to be fearful and isolate ourselves, dimming the light of unconditional love. It's needed more than ever. We can make it shine brighter than ever by keeping our hearts secure in God's marvelous love. If we want our roots to grow deeper and stronger, we have to be diligent about staying close to Him. Only then will we understand how immovable perfect love is and how invaluable it is to share it with others.

Jesus said, "'You must love the LORD your God with all your heart, all your soul, and all your mind.' This is the first and greatest commandment. A second is equally important: 'Love your neighbor as yourself'" (Matthew 22:37-39 NLT). The greatest commandments are love-centered. There's nothing on this earth that matters more than loving God first. Having that in place puts everything else in perspective—and makes every relationship in our lives a priority.

Loving You is the way I learn to love others, Lord.
My desire is to deepen that love every day.

THE BEST WAY

Be humble and gentle.

EPHESIANS 4:2 TLB

With progress comes pressure. As technology races forward, it paints the illusion that our lives are less stressful because everything can be done more efficiently and with greater ease. All the while the world feels a collective need to slow down. Having nearly everything doable at our fingertips through our phones, we miss what makes life worth living—the people in them. God designed the best way to the best life, and it highlights building and nurturing relationships. Humility and gentleness have sadly given way to competitiveness and hurried or harsh responses. We can't be in a rush twelve hours a day and expect to have a fulfilling life. We can't have our minds weighted with worry and work demands and expect to be humble and gentle with the people around us. Putting our phones down pulls our eyes, hearts, and minds upward. We're able to simply be present.

When we're present with our people, God is pleased. Love is ignited. Peace starts to surface. All the good things God intended come into focus. It's a gift to be humble and gentle, because they're by-products of love—and filling the world with love will take us to a better place than technology ever will.

Keep my eyes on the prize, Lord.
Yours is the love people need to see through me.

Your strength
must come from
the Lord's mighty
power within you.

EPHESIANS 6:10 TLB

LEAVING ROOM

Be patient with each other,
making allowance for each other's faults
because of your love.

EPHESIANS 4:2 TLB

L ove as the driving force in everything we do develops patience in us and grows the capacity of our grace to forgive. Love encourages us to increase the "allowance" we afford the people in our lives. When we make allowances for each other's faults, we leave ample room for love to expand. We're fallible humans in a broken world serving an infallible God who has infinite compassion. Only because of His unwavering love are we able to operate in love at all times. It takes a lot of thought-capturing, deep-breath-taking, and pause-before-responding on our part, but that's how we learn to allow the Holy Spirit to prevail. Jesus said, "The Helper, the Holy Spirit, whom the Father will send in My name, He will teach you all things, and bring to your remembrance all things that I said to you" (John 14:26 NKJV).

"What would Jesus do?" should be more than a catchy slogan in our lives—it should be a question we're able to answer by the power of the Holy Spirit. At all times, in every situation, and with every person, God has given us the power to let love be in control. What an amazing gift for which we can be continually grateful!

Give me a quiet mind and a sensitive heart, Lord,
so that Your lead is all that I listen to.

EVERY PIECE
IN PLACE

Live full lives, full in the fullness of God.

EPHESIANS 3:19 THE MESSAGE

When we're filled with God, the overflow is love. Love leads to the most fulfilling life—it's why we were created and what we were created to do. Love is the path to every heart, armed with the power to change it. Nothing else we say or do makes more of a difference than love will. Listen quietly. Smile widely. Hug tightly. Speak kindly. Serve humbly. There are endless ways to love people and simple ways to show it. Love has an amazing ability to awaken a person to their worth and purpose—priceless things bestowed on us by a perfect God.

When we give or experience love, it resonates with the deepest part of us, because life is meant to be shared. We're better together. Family, friends, neighbors, coworkers, and every God-appointed connection makes our lives full and meaningful. His plan is detailed and indestructible, built on our relationship with Him and each other. We sometimes think we need to figure out the pattern of our lives and what we should be doing, when in truth, it's always right in front of us—Jesus said, "Love each other. Just as I have loved you, you should love each other" (John 13:34 NLT). In doing this, every piece falls into place more beautifully than we can imagine.

Increase in me the capacity to love and give grace
to everyone in my life, Lord.

A CONSTANT EXPRESSION

When I think of the wisdom and scope of His plan,
I fall down on my knees and pray.

❧ EPHESIANS 3:14 TLB ❧

Precious Lord, take my hand; lead me on, let me stand; I am tired, I am weak, I am worn—a lyric written by Thomas A. Dorsey in 1932 is as relevant today as it has ever been. This world is a difficult place; the darkness is real; and trusting in the wisdom of God's plan tests our faith in mighty ways. When we stand reminded that the scope of His plan is far greater than we can comprehend, our wisest response is prayer—a falling-down, bended-knee, heartfelt prayer for the strength to put love into action despite our growing fears and a mounting temptation to retreat. It can become comfortable to cocoon. It can seem logical to lie low. It can feel safer to isolate. So we must remember this: "As for God, His way is perfect; the word of the LORD is proven; He is a shield to all who trust in Him" (II Samuel 22:31 NKJV).

God's perfect way is to love others. God's plan is for us to be together. His presence is promised, His power is predominant, and His purpose is fulfilled when we lift up one another. God never intended for us to travel alone—love is to be shared and shown—and we are called to be its constant expression.

Give me courage today, Lord,
to love without hesitation.

LACKING NOTHING

Now we can come fearlessly
right into God's presence, assured of His glad welcome
when we come with Christ and trust in Him.

❧ EPHESIANS 3:12 TLB ❧

Preparation is key to winning any battle we face. Going fearlessly into the presence of God will keep our hearts fearless when the going gets tough in our lives. And tough it will be at times. None of us are exempt from challenges, and many are fraught with suffering and pain. Yet we're encouraged to "count it all joy when you fall into various trials, knowing that the testing of your faith produces patience. But let patience have its perfect work, that you may be perfect and complete, lacking nothing" (James 1:2-4 NKJV).

Imagine arriving at the place where we lack nothing we need to live a perfectly peaceful, patient life, trusting God in any circumstance. Our humanness often gives way to emotions, but that's when we reach out to our spiritual mentors, our supportive friends, and our loving families. Any one of them is a gift from

God, fellow sojourners in God's love story for each of us. Just as we're not above suffering, we're not above needing the help God gives through the people in our lives. Each time we trust in Him, we get closer to being complete—lacking nothing by letting nothing shake our faith.

I come to You fearlessly, Lord.
I trust every circumstance is an opportunity
to trust You more.

INFALLIBLE

May you be able to feel and understand,
as all God's children should, how long,
how wide, how deep, and how high
His love really is.

> EPHESIANS 3:18 TLB

God loves us when the darkness is longer than we feared it would be. God loves us when the hurt leaves a wound wider than we think we can bear. God loves us when the valley is lower than we worried it would be and when the mountain is higher than we expected. God's love really is unconditional and beyond understanding. It's always active but not always felt.

Paul's prayer for us to be able to feel and understand the infinite love of our Father was spoken from a heart swelled with hope. It was preceded by a prayer that our roots would dig deeper into the truth of God's love, be watered by His Word, and remain anchored in His grace. We're on a lifelong adventure in the hands of a sovereign God. Our purpose is to learn to love Him more and more so we become the hands, feet, and voice of His love and grace in this challenging world. We'll have times when we feel His love, and we'll have times when in reflection, we understand His love. In all things, at all times, the hope is that we'll trust God no matter what—because perfect love is an infallible guide.

Your love is my anchor and authority, Lord.
Increase my understanding and build my trust.

REAL JOY

Under His direction, the whole body
is fitted together perfectly, and each part
in its own special way helps the other parts,
so that the whole body is healthy
and growing and full of love.

EPHESIANS 4:15–16 TLB

We are intricately unique creations. Each of us has a special, irreplaceable part to play in filling the world with love. In His wisdom, God designed our lives to fit together perfectly, taking into consideration our individual qualities, strengths, and even our weaknesses. Knowing God sees our lives from beginning to end leaves no room or time to question His choices. Under His direction, we are perfectly in place. Even when there are people who test our patience, jobs that stretch our faith, wilderness walks that weary our trust, or moments when we're pushed to the limit of our human emotions. . .we're right where God wants us to be. The quicker we surrender and humble ourselves before Him, the sooner our eyes are opened to the real joy in anywhere He chooses for us—

He's growing us for greater things.

The greatest thing of all is a life full of love. When our life is committed to helping others and using our gifts for His glory, we're not only in the perfect place, we're following His perfect will.

Direct my steps today, Lord.
Let each one be taken with joy and humility.

SET APART

Let me say this, then, speaking for the Lord:
Live no longer as the unsaved do, for they are blinded
and confused. Their closed hearts are full of darkness;
they are far away from the life of God.

➢• EPHESIANS 4:17-18 TLB •◄

The life of God is the light that sets us apart in a world where darkness rears its ugly head. A single newscast on any given day can replace faith with fear and hope with a feeling of helplessness. While media outlets shine the spotlight on everything that's going wrong, the life of the One who makes everything right lives within us.

"Don't hide your light! Let it shine for all; let your good deeds glow for all to see, so that they will praise your heavenly Father" (Matthew 5:15-16 TLB). The world needs to see the life we lead—one of love, compassion, kindness, and generosity. The difference we make lasts because of the difference Jesus makes in us. Living for Him means lifting Him up in everything we do, letting the light of God's love dispel the darkness. The more love, the brighter our lives and the better our world. Today won't lack opportunities to help someone, be there for a friend, or let our loving actions point people to God. We need only be willing, glowing, good-deed-doers for His glory.

I want to live a life that magnifies You, Lord. Let all I do bring praise to You.

A SMALL THING

Do not let any unwholesome talk
come out of your mouths, but only what is helpful
for building others up according to their needs,
that it may benefit those who listen.

➤ **EPHESIANS 4:29 NIV** ◆

Our choice of words is one of the most powerful things we have—and maybe the most difficult to discipline. "The tongue is a small thing, but what enormous damage it can do" (James 3:5 TLB).

In contrast, what incredible good it can do when we use words to encourage others, build them up, or speak truth to searching hearts. When words of kindness and love come out of our mouths, there's no way of measuring the positive impact they'll have on those who hear them.

Words matter. Every single one we give voice to affects the hearer, and it's wise to remember that we're one of them. Our words set our attitude, our outlook, and our outcomes. We can't consistently allow unwholesome talk, unkind responses, or ungrateful thoughts to flow out of our mouths and expect God's blessing, favor, and abundant life to unfold. Putting those gifts in motion requires us to know the truth and say it out loud. Psalm 103:20 (NKJV) says, "Bless the LORD, you His angels, who excel in strength, who do His word, heeding the voice of His word." God's Word is alive—and His angels stand ready to change lives when they hear it.

Give me wisdom and discernment when I speak, Lord.

PRAYERFULLY PICKING UP

God wants us to grow up,
to know the whole truth and tell it in love—
like Christ in everything.

EPHESIANS 4:14 THE MESSAGE

Being unshakably confident that we're whole in Christ—needing no person, possession, or position to fulfill us—is the only way to act like Him in everything we say and do. In a world where nearly everything we need to manage our daily lives can be accomplished from a device in the palm of our hands, it's tempting to think we're in control. It can be easy to believe we've "got this" without the involvement of our Savior—and we couldn't be more deceived. His constant involvement in our lives is the conduit for consistently bringing the love and truth of God to the people around us. There's nothing we need more.

Growing up spiritually has a great deal to do with laying down our own way of doing things every day to prayerfully pick up His. The result will be loving people and living selflessly. Putting Jesus first and acknowledging our desperate need for Him every day anchors our spirits in the truth that without Him, we're not who we could or should be. He is our wholeness— and this world can offer only empty, counterfeit substitutes.

I want to be wholly aware of You, Lord.
Let everything I do be a reflection of You.

STRENGTHENING TIES

*If you have really heard His voice
and learned from Him the truths concerning Himself,
then throw off your old evil nature.*

EPHESIANS 4:21–22 TLB

It feels good to throw away, or give away, material things we no longer find useful or beautiful. Routinely purging our possessions clears out the excess and unwanted, leaving space and light for what's most important to us. It's good to sometimes reflect on our old nature—the one we "threw away" when we accepted the One who became most important to us. Learning the truth about Jesus and what He taught creates space and light in our lives for loving people. With Him, it's never about achievements, accolades, or annual income. It's always about relationships.

Apart from one another, we tend to develop tunnel vision concerning our lives, focusing on success over friendships, possessions over people, and curb appeal over the needs of our neighbors. Together we strengthen our ties to our Creator. He made us for one another, and He knows we need to stay connected. The world is a clever and cunning distraction. . .and this is a critical time to really hear God's voice and learn.

My heart's desire is to focus on the people in my life, and those You bring into it, Lord. Show me ways to speak and serve so that You are what they see.

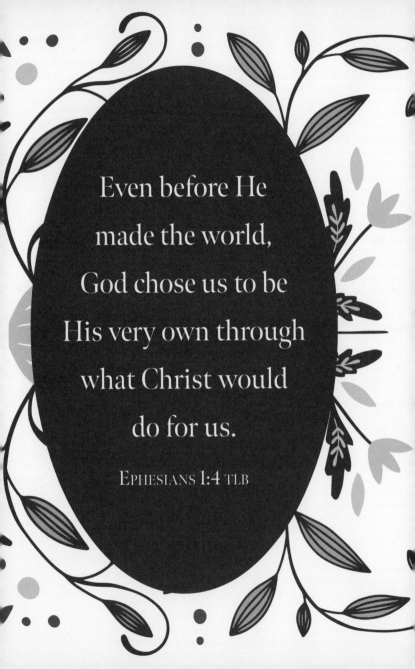

Even before He made the world, God chose us to be His very own through what Christ would do for us.

EPHESIANS 1:4 TLB

CONNECTED

Now your attitudes and thoughts
must all be constantly changing for the better.

EPHESIANS 4:23 TLB

In life, change is inevitable. The changes aren't always welcomed or what we'd choose, but they're no surprise to God. That's why our attitudes and thoughts must all be constantly changing for the better. We will be brokenhearted. We will suffer loss. We will experience pain we hoped we wouldn't. Still, our attitude must be one of obstinate trust in God. We have to stubbornly refuse to become bitter, being fully convinced that God saw the changes before they got here and provided His love to power us through.

While God understands our human emotions—Jesus felt all of them—the moment we hurt, He closes in. "The Lord is close to the brokenhearted and saves those who are crushed in spirit" (Psalm 34:18 NIV). When we're crushed in spirit, falling helplessly beneath the weight of unthinkable tragedy, betrayal, or circumstances beyond our control, God's hand is already in place to catch us. As He is to us in our darkest times, we can be to others in theirs. As we grow more confident in His comfort than ever before, more sure of His strength in our weakness, God will call on us to be the arms that lift others. All we go through connects us... and carries us ever closer to Him.

Open my eyes, hands, and heart to those who are hurting, Lord. Make me a vessel of Your love.

SLOWING THE PACE

Walk worthy of the calling with which
you were called, with all lowliness and gentleness,
with long-suffering, bearing with one another in love.

EPHESIANS 4:1–2 NKJV

At the pace of this world—hurried, scheduled, pressured—we can get to a place where we're racing forward, missing any chance to see each other's needs. But what if we took the time to slow down and learn to walk again? To walk worthy of our calling requires patience, humility, and a quieter, gentler speed. Have you ever noticed how much more clearly you see details when you take a walk versus a bike ride. . .or a bike ride versus a drive? The same can be said about seeing the faces of people— the sadness in their eyes, the broken smiles, and the downcast souls. As we race through our days, they become a blur. If we don't see them, God can't move in our hearts to love them.

So many things can wait, but the needs of others often cannot. There's urgency in the prayer asking

God for a glimpse of hope in the midst of heartache. There's necessity in the prayer asking God for provision. There's desperation in the prayer asking God to show them His love is alive and present. Bearing with one another in love means being the hands and feet of God. . .and there's nothing more worthy of our time.

As Your children, we need one another, Lord.
Show me where Your love is most needed today.

A PERFECT WHOLE

Tell the truth, for we are parts of each other.

> EPHESIANS 4:25 TLB

Fear can make us doubt what we know and say what we shouldn't. To avoid rejection, hurting another person, or facing the repercussions of a bad choice, we sometimes avoid being truthful. Lies and half-truths lead to regret and disappointment. Paul felt compelled to encourage believers to speak truth with our neighbors (see Ephesians 4:25 NKJV) because being dishonest compromises our unity with one another and with God. Love and kindness bind us. Truth and forgiveness unite us. Mercy mends us.

When the sun comes up on a new day, it brings with it another chance to repair broken relationships, to accept and offer mercy, and to embark on the path of healing. It's important for us to be honest with ourselves and transparent in our conversations with God. Personal accountability and self-forgiveness clear the way for us to love and forgive the people in our lives.

God is a loving Father who will always show us where we need His strength and how we need to grow. "The faithful love of the LORD never ends! His mercies never cease. Great is His faithfulness; His mercies begin afresh each morning" (Lamentations 3:22-23 NLT). God in His perfect love has called us to be part of a perfect whole—patterned together in His never-ending grace.

Give me courage to tell the truth without fear,
Lord, so that unity and love thrives.

IN GOD'S HAND

Say only what helps, each word a gift.

EPHESIANS 4:29 THE MESSAGE

Words as gifts. . .what a beautiful thought. They cost nothing to give and take little effort to express, yet they have the power to change someone's life or set the course of their day. If we pay attention and look closely, we can see how a kind word washes over the countenance of the one to whom we're speaking, literally lighting up their face. In today's world, kind words are more valuable than we realize. How do we keep that truth in the forefront of our minds? Practice.

Kindness, essentially giving voice to God's love, is habit-forming. What would happen if—when a kind thought comes into our minds, we said it? Or when a kind deed comes into our mind while we pray, we did it? The more often we follow through when God prompts us, the more likely we are to keep doing so. Less hesitation leads to more love. God is looking for willing and obedient vessels through which to pour

His love, and this is no time to let our lives sit on the shelf. We need to be in God's hands, ready to be used for His purposes. "For it is God who works in you both to will and to do for His good pleasure" (Philippians 2:13 NKJV).

Let Your love flow through me freely today, Lord.
Give me words filled with love and light.

LOVE IN MOTION

Be imitators of God as dear children.

>· EPHESIANS 5:1 NKJV ·<

When we act like God, we look like love. We're the one walking to our neighbor's house to help them with a project. We're the one making dinner for a family going through a hard time. We're the one writing an encouraging note to a friend or providing companion care for the elderly. We're the one who smiles at others, opens doors, offers a kindness, and prays without ceasing. Every act of love can initiate a reaction of gratefulness and praise for our Father, and without fail, it sets the power of His love in motion. "For the Holy Spirit, God's gift, does not want you to be afraid of people, but to be wise and strong, and to love them" (II Timothy 1:7 TLB).

Love in motion will change the world. It draws hearts to our Savior, transforms heartache to hope, and inspires a ripple effect of good things. It's the best investment we can make because we're depositing the goodness of God in the lives of people—His crowning creation. Seeing us come together to help each other through life makes God smile big. Together we're strong, hopeful, and increasingly confident in our faith. Together, we fulfill the first and second commandments at once—love God, love people.

I'm created in Your image, Lord.
Show me how to be more like You every day.

AN UNWANTED HARVEST

Don't use your anger as fuel for revenge.
And don't stay angry.

EPHESIANS 4:26 THE MESSAGE

Wrangling our anger can be difficult, especially if we're tempted to feel justified in harboring it after being treated unfairly or with disrespect. The harvest of staying angry is bitterness and division—neither of which are pleasing to God. Life will present a parade of challenges in this area. The sooner we learn to diffuse our angry, negative feelings toward others by releasing the offense to God in prayer, the quicker we maintain love's control. The faster we forgive, the fuller our lives will be. Jesus is our Teacher. In the moment He was mocked and treated more unfairly than we will ever be, His response was, "Father, forgive them, for they do not know what they do" (Luke 23:34 NKJV).

Relinquishing our control will restore our right standing with God. "Your heavenly Father will forgive you if you forgive those who sin against you; but if you refuse to forgive them, He will not forgive you" (Matthew 6:14-15 TLB). It couldn't be more striking or straightforward. Apart from God, it's impossible to love one another in truth. Anger accompanied by unforgiveness keeps the dividing wall in place—with humility, surrender, and love, we daily tear it down.

*I surrender to You, Lord,
and ask for love to guide my words
and actions at all times.*

A LIFE OF JOY

It is God Himself who has made us
what we are and given us new lives
from Christ Jesus; and long ages ago
He planned that we should spend these lives
in helping others.

⇒• EPHESIANS 2:10 TLB •⇐

God's plan for each of us is unique in many
ways, but in one way it is always the same—to
spend our lives helping others. It was His plan for us
before we took our first breath, because He knew
our journeys would be blessed as a result. Helping
others keeps our focus on love and every definition
of it: "Love suffers long and is kind; love does not
envy; love does not parade itself, is not puffed up;
does not behave rudely, does not seek its own, is not
provoked, thinks no evil; does not rejoice in iniquity,
but rejoices in the truth" (I Corinthians 13:4–6 NKJV).

Helping one another glorifies God and reminds
us what a celebration that is. It cultivates a deep joy in
us, one that's secured in Him and hard to uproot. The

world runs from one popular trend to another seeking a sustainable joy, to no avail. Seeking to live a life of love that mirrors the life of Jesus is the only way to fill our days with joy. . .and fulfill God's plan for our lives.

You planned for me to live my life helping others, Lord. Show me that my greatest joy is found in Your desire.

FIT TOGETHER

There is one body and one Spirit,
just as you were called in one hope of your calling;
one Lord, one faith, one baptism;
one God and Father of all, who is above all,
and through all, and in you all.

EPHESIANS 4:4–6 NKJV

There is no separation in the body of Christ. We are one. Fit together for His glory, each of us has a special part to play in the lives we touch, the places we live, the jobs we do, and the family we're given. Every day brings new opportunities to magnify every reason God has put us together the way that He has. There are no flaws in His design for our lives. Even in times when we feel like we don't belong where we are, being asked to do things we don't want to do, we can be certain God is doing some trust building.

When we face our challenges with a positive attitude and without murmuring or complaining, we learn humility in a lasting way. We grow up in

God. We start to see the people in front of us as the ones God chose for us to serve with a spirit of love. He doesn't make mistakes. . .He molds hearts into the likeness of Christ.

Thank You for the people You chose for my life, Lord. Let me be a beacon of love and grace for each one.

LOOKING GOOD

You must be a new and different person,
holy and good. Clothe yourself
with this new nature.

EPHESIANS 4:24 TLB

New and different. . .holy and good. When we look back on who we were and how we were before giving our lives to Christ, we understand that becoming a new and different person is a divine and priceless gift. "If anyone is in Christ, the new creation has come. The old has gone, the new is here!" (II Corinthians 5:17 NIV). Clothing ourselves with this new nature looks like being there for our friends and families. It looks like loving the unlovable and serving the lost. It looks selfless, kind, humble, and hopeful. The outside presentation of our inside purification in Christ should look different to the world in the best kind of way. Our lives should stand out because of whose we are, not who we are, and not because of big achievements, but because of small gestures.

Quietly giving our time and resources continually—in countless kindnesses every day and in measures seen as miraculous answers from an attentive God—is the way we're called to live. Being on this journey together means focusing on our oneness with Christ. He is the way love becomes light. He is the way life becomes whole. He is the way our reflection becomes the difference the world needs to see.

Clothe me in Your love and grace today, Lord.
Let my words and actions make a lasting difference.

THE HELPER

Don't grieve God. Don't break His heart.
His Holy Spirit, moving and breathing in you,
is the most intimate part of your life,
making you fit for Himself.
Don't take such a gift for granted.

 EPHESIANS 4:30 THE MESSAGE

The Holy Spirit, our best Friend, Helper, and Comforter, is the most intimate part of our lives, a gift we can never take for granted. He brings to life the character of God in us, teaching us at all times the way we should act and react, the words we should speak, and the way we should treat others. We can't love the people around us without surrendering to the life within us. God's love in us is a constant reminder that we need each other to travel through this world in the way we were created to. With a humble dependence on God, we willingly help each other, which is the fulfillment of His plan for humankind. Isolation short-circuits the work the Holy Spirit is here to accomplish in our lives. "The

Friend, the Holy Spirit whom the Father will send at My request, will make everything plain to you. He will remind you of all the things I have told you" (John 14:26 THE MESSAGE). Everything Jesus said is what the Holy Spirit reminds us to do—we need only be increasingly good listeners.

Sharpen my spiritual hearing, Lord,
so that all I do is pleasing to You.

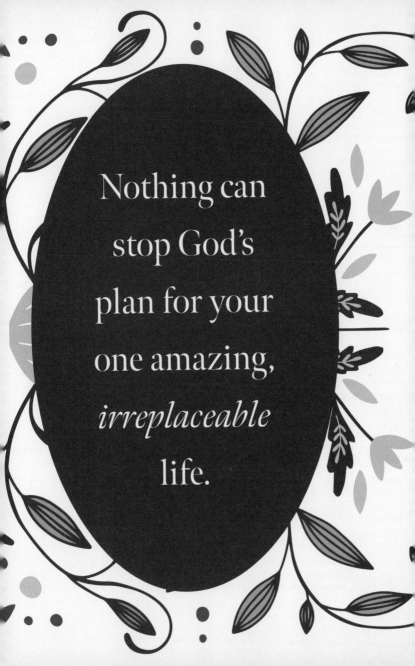

Nothing can
stop God's
plan for your
one amazing,
irreplaceable
life.

THE FLOW OF FORGIVENESS

Be kind to one another,
tenderhearted, forgiving one another,
even as God in Christ forgave you.

> **EPHESIANS 4:32 NKJV** ·

Life is hard, and sometimes the pressures can bear down and smother our tenderness toward one another. In our hearts, we want to be kind and forgiving, but in our humanness and emotional distress, we shorten the fuse to impatience and frustration. Our responses stray from the love and forgiveness we know and need, leading to the guilt and regret we don't need. We're fallible. We make mistakes. But never should we allow our moments of weakness to create walls. We must go to the Father for forgiveness, then to the ones we've sinned against—and the sooner, the better.

Life is challenging, but it's also fleeting. We don't have time to spend on severed relationships, with God or with each other. We need the flow of forgiveness to remain wide open. When Jesus taught us how to pray to the Father, He included, "Forgive us our sins, as we have forgiven those who sin against us" (Matthew 6:12 NLT). We ask for forgiveness and offer forgiveness, while the river of grace runs through our lives bringing love, peace, kindness, and tenderness. And when the sun rises again, filled with new mercies, we gratefully receive them with arms open wide.

Thank You for the grace to get me through the day, Lord. I welcome Your mercies every morning.

IN STEP WITH EACH OTHER

We take our lead from Christ,
who is the source of everything we do.
He keeps us in step with each other.

EPHESIANS 4:15 The Message

Just as God knit us together in our mothers' wombs, in His perfect plan He put us together with the people in our lives. God guides our steps to the places we go and to the people we're meant to meet, each having a purpose within our purpose. When we understand His uninterrupted involvement in everything that affects us, we get better at accepting, with grateful hearts, every choice He makes. There is a reason for every season. From the times of suffering to the times of rejoicing and every moment in between, Christ is the Source of everything we do. With His loving leadership, we learn to trust God no matter what and to prayerfully build our relationships with one another. Our personal relationships are the most important things in our lives, and they're orchestrated by Him. Whether for our spiritual growth, for our physical provision, or to share the gifts He's given us to help each other, God makes no mistakes in connecting us. His hand is our perfect guide. . .His heart our perfect lead.

I want to see Your purpose
in all my relationships, Lord. Give me wisdom
to follow Your lead and be grateful,
gracious, and kind.

THE CLEAREST REFLECTION

Take on an entirely new way of life—
a God-fashioned life, a life renewed from the inside
and working itself into your conduct as God
accurately reproduces His character in you.

EPHESIANS 4:24 The Message

Renewal takes time. It takes discipline, perseverance, and prioritizing. Putting God first, always, is our only hope of becoming the clearest possible reflection of His love in this world. It requires us to remember that we need His truth to live in His likeness.

"Do not conform to the pattern of this world, but be transformed by the renewing of your mind. Then you will be able to test and approve what God's will is—His good, pleasing, and perfect will" (Romans 12:2 NIV). Unfortunately, it's easy to conform to the pattern of the world. It's filled with endless duties and countless distractions, shallow solutions offering temporal fulfillment, and a constant pressure to compromise the truth. We can get used to being comfortable and stray from Christ, our Comforter and Compass. Yet God knows our transformation takes time and happens from the inside out. As we read His Word, He renews our way of thinking, which is then reflected in our actions. In time, the living Word becomes the life we live—a life centered in His good, pleasing, and perfect will.

Make my heart become like Yours, Lord.
Let Your living Word be my greatest pursuit and joy.

DRAWN TOGETHER

*When you are angry,
you give a mighty foothold
to the devil.*

EPHESIANS 4:27 TLB

In an environment of division and unrest, retreat is a viable temptation. We can believe that security is found in a home we create, a smaller circle of people we invite into our lives, or a comfortable routine that allows little room for listening to God's still, small voice. The truth is, there is no security outside of Jesus Christ.

Jesus surrendered to every step God directed Him to take, knowing each one bound His life securely to God's will—the highest purpose of our earthly journeys. Investing our time, resources, and prayers in the lives of others not only honors God but reveals His heart to the world. Rising above our differences helps us see the real and deepest need of every human. Love is the life-changer. Love reaches over walls and is louder than any argument. Love defies all odds and is seen clearer than any slogan. Love draws us together when everything else in this world tries to pull us apart. God chose us to be givers—not of anger, catchy comebacks, or powerful points—but of love that is as present and as unconditional as His.

Give me the wisdom and strength to put love first,
Lord, no matter how I feel.
I surrender to serving You
in every way You ask me to.

FIT TOGETHER
BY LOVE

His very breath and blood flow through us,
nourishing us so that we will grow up
healthy in God, robust in love.

EPHESIANS 4:16 THE MESSAGE

Our next breath depends on God. "In Him we live and move and have our being" (Acts 17:28 NIV). The same power that rolled away the stone and resurrected Jesus is flowing through us. The life of God in us is how we live fulfilled, at peace, and with purpose. A grown-up life with God in control is constantly looking outward to the needs of others. Where can we serve? How can we help? Whom can we love?

We've gotten to a place when spoken communication is avoided for the sake of time because a text is quick and easy. But there's comfort in hearing a voice when we're hurting. God wired us to depend on each other to build our faith and boost our courage. A conversation, a hug, a walk, a lunch date, or simply being physically present are ways to manifest God's love. We're alive and together at this place in time for reasons uniquely written in His story for our lives. Our families, friends, and neighbors are pieces of a beautiful whole—fit together by a perfect love.

Your love is my goal and my guide, Lord.
Teach me to move through my days with
a heart ready to reflect every good thing in You.

TOGETHER WE LEARN

Be gentle with one another, sensitive.

EPHESIANS 4:31 The Message

Haste and hurry can contribute to our being insensitive and unkind. Pressure coming from any part of our lives pushes us to our limits emotionally, sometimes without us realizing it. That is, until we say or do something we regret. "The fruit of the Spirit is love, joy, peace, longsuffering, kindness, goodness, faithfulness, gentleness, self-control" (Galatians 5:22–23 NKJV). How we treat others reveals who's in control of our spirit at the moment—and we never want that to be anyone but the Holy Spirit.

When we choose separation and isolation through anger or offenses, it prevents love from thriving. When we feel ourselves getting to a place that keeps us from acting in a gentle, sensitive way, we need to pause and walk away. It's better to take a step back than to create a split. Our relationships are more important than anything else in our lives. Lasting connections are sustained by loving actions, kind words, and thoughtful responses. Life is too short to spend our days on anything other than appreciating the gift of the people God has given us. Together, we learn the value of peace, longsuffering, self-control, and love. . .and through them the overwhelming goodness of God.

I pray for every fruit of the Spirit to be present in me, Lord, so others see the beauty of You.

A POWERFUL GIFT

If you are angry, don't sin by nursing your grudge.
Don't let the sun go down with you still angry—
get over it quickly.

> EPHESIANS 4:26 TLB

By definition, a grudge is a persistent feeling of ill will or resentment resulting from a past insult or injury. Ouch. There couldn't be a more opposite definition of the grace of God. Anger, if not managed and released, can become a deep-seated, dark spot within us that becomes harder to remove with time. God understands this, and that's why His Word instructs us to let go of our anger before the sun sets on our day. It's a sin to hold on to it. . .and in turn, we're set free by releasing it.

It might take a little time for our feelings to line up with our decision, but the decision has to be made nonetheless. And the truth is, "the more we see our sinfulness, the more we see God's abounding grace forgiving us" (Romans 5:20 TLB). We forgive and let go because we've been forgiven, time and time again. Staying mindful and grateful for the grace we're given helps us forgive others more quickly. The more we sharpen our quick-release skills when it comes to being angry, the more energy we have for loving the people around us—and that's a powerful gift to bring to every sunrise.

Keep my focus on Your grace, Lord,
so I'm quick to forgive.

THE BEST COMPANY

*Watch what God does, and then you do it,
like children who learn proper behavior
from their parents. . .Keep company with Him
and learn a life of love.*

EPHESIANS 5:1 THE MESSAGE

The best way for us to be the best company for others is to keep company with God. We can't let ourselves feel defeated or upset if our way of doing that isn't exactly like everyone we know, read about, or look up to—because there isn't a single moment in our twenty-four-hour day that God is apart from us. Not one. An attainable habit for all of us is to follow Paul's instruction to "pray without ceasing" (I Thessalonians 5:17 NKJV). God knows the silent requests of our hearts, and He sees the struggles coming before we face them. Jesus encouraged us to "remember, your Father knows exactly what you need even before you ask Him!" (Matthew 6:8 TLB).

Being able to have an ongoing conversation with God throughout our waking hours is the greatest privilege of our lives. Inviting Him into every decision we make, every relationship we have, and every challenge we encounter is the wisest way to learn from Him, love Him, and live in His likeness. Binding our hearts and thoughts to God in constant communication builds a life of confident faith. . .and reveals, through us, an unstoppable hope.

Thank You for being my constant companion, Lord, and guiding me with wisdom and love.

LOVE AND UNITY

Forgive one another as quickly and thoroughly
as God in Christ forgave you.

EPHESIANS 4:32 THE MESSAGE

Forgiving one another can be hard. God created our emotions for beautiful reasons, but left unchecked and uncontrolled, the duo of anger and unforgiveness are harmful companions. The longer we allow them to simmer in our heart and mind, the more difficult it is to surrender them to God and begin healing. Forgiving one another quickly and thoroughly is wise advice that we need to practice and perfect if we're going to experience true peace. There's nothing more necessary if we hope to fulfill God's purpose for our lives. Love and unity depend on it.

"Christ became a human being and lived here on earth among us and was full of loving forgiveness" (John 1:14 TLB). Following the example of Jesus keeps us filled with love for each other, in spite of our feelings, our faults, and our failures. Being in a continual mindset of gentleness, humility, and kindness prepares our heart to be at the ready to forgive. Colossians 3:13 (TLB) tells us to "be gentle and ready to forgive; never hold grudges." Gratefully remembering the grace God has given us is the way to forgive others freely and fully—and to encourage togetherness through love.

Help me walk in Your gentle way, Lord,
and forgive with a humble, loving heart.

THE SWEETEST
SCENT

God was pleased, for Christ's love for you
was like a sweet perfume to Him.

EPHESIANS 5:2 TLB

God was pleased with Christ's love-driven sacrifice...but oh, how the event broke His heart. Restoring our relationship with the Father came with an emotional cost, yet the love in it rose like a sweet perfume into the heavens. It was a perfect scent from a perfect sacrifice. It's fitting that Paul used this simile to describe the unconditional love that led to the gift of grace. Our sense of smell is closely linked with memory, in a stronger way than any other sense God gave us. In studies, people often say that the sense of smell evokes memories so well that they feel as if they're experiencing the event again.

In a way, Paul tells us God will not forget what was given in order to restore us to eternal life in His presence—nor should we forget. The reunion could happen by no other way, and it reflected the priceless love Jesus has for both us and the Father. Imagine the smell of sweet perfume wafting through heaven as a constant reminder that the price has been paid for our sin and no further payment is needed. Unity and love are at the center of God's heart. . .and Jesus showed us the infinite value of both.

Thank You, Lord, for reuniting us with the Father through a love beyond our comprehension.

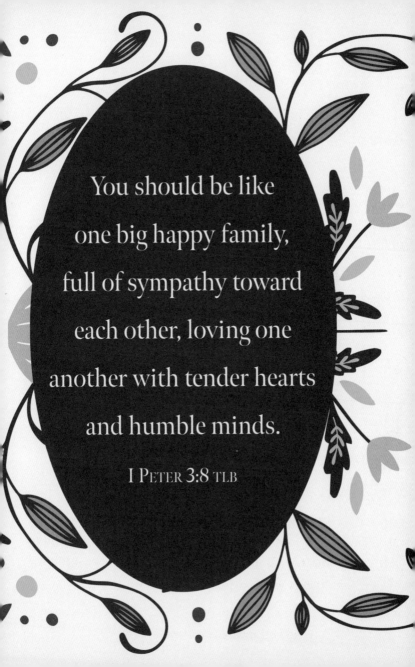

You should be like
one big happy family,
full of sympathy toward
each other, loving one
another with tender hearts
and humble minds.

I Peter 3:8 TLB

NURTURING TOGETHERNESS

Be full of love for others,
following the example of Christ
who loved you and gave Himself to God
as a sacrifice to take away your sins.

◆ EPHESIANS 5:2 TLB ◆

When we set our minds on being full of love for others, there's room for little else. It's habit-forming. Our thoughts can be stopped, taken captive, and tossed out if they seek to send us in any other direction than love. Philippians 4:8 (NLT) says, "Fix your thoughts on what is true, and honorable, and right, and pure, and lovely, and admirable. Think about things that are excellent and worthy of praise." Thought-capturing is a discipline that nurtures togetherness and destroys division.

What we allow our minds to dwell on affects our actions. Harboring unforgiveness and holding on to hurts only hurts us. Redirecting our mental energy to things we can do to build the relationships in our lives and how we can help the people God brings into our lives will increase our joy exponentially! Love is always the path to positive outcomes. Being generous with love is always the way to grow godly friendships, bless our neighbors, and make a stranger in need feel valued by God. The opportunities are in front of us every day—we just need to fill our minds with praiseworthy thoughts and open our hearts with Christlike love.

Bring my thoughts in line with truth, Lord,
and let my life be a constant reflection of Your love.

SHIFTING FOCUS

Remind each other of God's goodness,
and be thankful.

>• EPHESIANS 5:4 TLB •<

Spending time with people we love and those who need to be encouraged by love is the best way to live our lives well. Even though we're busy and bound by obligations of work, household duties, appointments, and errands, balance is essential—and prayer helps us keep it. God wants us to be together to remind each other how faithful He's been to us in different circumstances, trials, and difficult seasons. Retreat and reclusion can seem easier and more manageable when we're fighting life's battles, but it brings heartache, and most importantly, it opposes God's plan.

Woven into each of us is the need for connection. When we're tempted to recoil from people, we risk trapping ourselves in a pattern God never intended for us. We're created to do life together. . .side by side, day by day. The beauty of looking into the face of someone who's encouraging us, or needing encouragement, brings a necessary shift in focus. We turn our thoughts upward, not inward. Our hearts start to feel thankful and hopeful, not downcast and doubtful. We praise God, saying, "My voice You shall hear in the morning, O LORD; in the morning I will direct it to You, and I will look up" (Psalm 5:3 NKJV). Loving people is the pinnacle of our purpose—and starting our day looking up will set our course in the right direction.

It's not about me, Lord, but looking to You.

LOVE FIRST

A greedy person is really an idol worshiper—
he loves and worships the good things of this life
more than God.

EPHESIANS 5:5 TLB

It's easy to get caught in the trap of comparison and competition. Caught in its deception, greed is a blinding glare. Without realizing it, we can feel satisfaction in our accomplishments and the things we acquire rather than in Christ alone. Maintaining a clear vision of what matters most requires putting people before possessions. God's will is a willingness to love first, without thought of gain or glory.

Knowing how unconditionally and infinitely we're loved should compel us to push and propel that love into the world around us by treasuring the people in front of us. We can't know every struggle that's going on in their hearts and minds, but we can be there with a warm hug and a listening ear. We can encourage them with a smile and a comforting word. We can sit with them and seek to understand what they're going through, offering truths God has shown us in our tough times. This life is not a race of individual successes but one of spiritual significance—because what we see is far less important than what we don't see. "The things which are seen are temporary, but the things which are not seen are eternal" (II Corinthians 4:18 NKJV).

Give me a willing heart and an open hand, Lord.
Show me how to love others with every chance given.

UNITED IN SONG

Sing songs from your heart to Christ.

EPHESIANS 5:19 THE MESSAGE

Music is a gift from God with a powerful ability to produce a positive attitude. It's impossible to be discouraged while we're singing! Praise erupts from a grateful heart, and a grateful heart is the key to joy. What is there to sing to Jesus about?

"The free gift of God is eternal life through Jesus Christ our Lord" (Romans 6:23 TLB).

"There is now no condemnation awaiting those who belong to Christ Jesus" (Romans 8:1 TLB).

"Since we are His children, we will share His treasures—for all God gives to His Son Jesus is now ours too" (Romans 8:17 TLB).

"God will meet all your needs according to the riches of His glory in Christ Jesus" (Philippians 4:19 NIV).

"Jesus died for you" (Colossians 1:23 TLB).

"Jesus the Son of God is our great High Priest who has gone to heaven itself to help us" (Hebrews 4:14 TLB).

"If you sin, there is someone to plead for you before the Father. His name is Jesus Christ, the One who is all that is good and who pleases God completely" (I John 2:1 TLB).

That's a lot to sing about. That's a lot to be thankful for. That's all we need to live a life of joy, peace, love, and hope. . .one heartfelt song of praise at a time.

Let my heart sing Your praises without ceasing, Lord.

THE GIFT OF FRIENDSHIP

Learn as you go along what pleases the Lord.

֎• EPHESIANS 5:10 TLB •֎

Life is a learning process until we take our last breath. The most important lessons given are those we learn through the guidance and friendship of the Holy Spirit. Because He is one with God, there's no question about the direction He gives. One of the wisest things we can do on our earthly journeys is to develop friendships with people who want to please the Lord as much as we do. "You use steel to sharpen steel, and one friend sharpens another" (Proverbs 27:17 THE MESSAGE). Good friends are good gifts that shouldn't be taken for granted. They're part of God's design to help us sharpen our love and forgiveness toward one another, to inspire us to practice being selfless, and to teach us the healing power of laughter and joy.

Every good gift comes from God, and each gift holds more good for deeper reasons than we might ever realize. God's love for us and His desire for us to live blessed, abundant lives is truly beyond our human understanding. He wants only what's best for us. . .and a huge part of His best is fulfilling our inherent need to run this race together. He created us with unique strengths to share along the way—it's up to us to reach out and steady one another with every step we take.

Teach me to nurture my friendships, Lord,
and glorify You in each one.

HERE AND NOW

Make the most of every opportunity
you have for doing good.

EPHESIANS 5:16 TLB

There will be seasons in our life when we're not happy about the place to which God has brought us. In those times, grumbling is often easier than gratefulness. Mumbling rolls off our tongues when quiet prayers should, and our attitudes need constant adjustment. The faster we fall to our knees in humility, no matter what our circumstance, the sooner we see how God is always working things together for a good outcome. Very often He puts us in situations for us to practice every opportunity to do good for someone else. That's the life that mirrors God, and it's the purpose each one of us is called to fulfill.

The challenges in our lives prepare our hearts for the future God sees and we don't. Surrendering to His choices builds a trust in us that's necessary if we're going to look at each day with a joyful spirit and a hopeful, expectant outlook. Knowing His perfect love is the motivation for where He leads us should settle any doubt we have about where we are, and it should encourage excitement for where we're going. Right now, in this place, for His purpose, we need to make the most of every opportunity we have for doing good—and look forward to seeing the good He'll bring out of it.

Thank You for lovingly leading me, Lord.
I trust all my days are in Your hands.

LET THERE BE LIGHT!

For though once your heart was full of darkness,
now it is full of light from the Lord,
and your behavior should show it!

EPHESIANS 5:8 TLB

The light Jesus brought when He took up residence in our hearts dispelled the darkness there and exposed things we would never have seen on our own. We were blinded to our self-centered ways, consumed by our own ambitions, and sadly unaware of how to truly love people. When the love of God shed the light of Christ on the deepest parts of us, we began to see our worth, understand our purpose, and look for ways to share His love with the world. Now our behavior is more reflective of God's image and should become clearer as we draw closer to Him.

When the world around us grows darker, the desire for us to become brighter increases. The light of Christ in us is the beacon of hope, and it shines when we're kind. It glows when we give to those in need. It beams when we love our neighbors, bring together our families, and gather with our friends to laugh, encourage one another, and talk about our amazing God. Let's join together to navigate the dark days of this life—and shine His light into the lives of every person who crosses our paths.

Let Your light change and guide me, Lord.

WITH RESPECT

Out of respect for Christ,
be courteously reverent to one another.

EPHESIANS 5:21 THE MESSAGE

The way we treat people. . .from our people, to the people we meet, to the people we encounter even briefly. . .reflects our relationship with, and respect for, Jesus. When He walked the path of humanity we're currently on, He was full of loving forgiveness. In our imperfection, we'll fall short time and again, but out of love and respect for our perfect example, Jesus, we should be in constant communion with Him in the hope of acting more and more like Him. We need His wisdom, patience, and insight to determine what those around us need and to understand how to love them best.

We are one-of-a-kind creations with unique personalities, strengths, and weaknesses. Being courteously reverent to every fellow human is the beginning of being Christlike in our witness to them. We don't need them to see us; we want them to see

Him. Love lets go of pride, makes way for humility, and moves forward in forgiveness. Love is the only way to point people to eternal life in Christ—it's our truest directional signal and the surest guide we have to give.

Give me a humble heart, a discerning mind, and a respectful attitude, Lord. Fill me with Your love for every person in my life.

LOVING PEOPLE WELL

Be filled with the Spirit.

> **EPHESIANS 5:18 NIV**

We've been given a powerful Helper, Friend, and Comforter. Our hope of looking like Jesus and loving like God depends on the gift of the Holy Spirit—and the sharpening of our listening skills. "The love of God has been poured out in our hearts by the Holy Spirit who was given to us" (Romans 5:5 NKJV).

The gift we have in the Holy Spirit is irreplaceable and invaluable if we're going to love people God's way. Becoming complacent in our communication with Him breaks down our ability to fill our minds with the things Jesus taught. But when we become disciplined to trust in the presence of the Holy Spirit, we learn to depend on Him for godly actions, reactions, and replies. He'll help us remember the words of Jesus and the ways of love. He'll inspire hope in us and deepen our confidence in God's love for us. God sent Him with an eternally embedded purpose in our lives. Ephesians 4:30 (TLB) says, "Don't cause the Holy Spirit sorrow by the way you live." Loving people well and living with divine decision-making abilities begins with our reliance on the Holy Spirit. . .the Spirit of truth within us.

Thank You for the Holy Spirit, Lord.
Your gifts are always good and perfect.

THE PRIVILEGE OF PRAYER

Pray hard and long.
Pray for your brothers and sisters.

EPHESIANS 6:17 THE MESSAGE

When we're praying for one another, there's no room for judgment, pointing fingers, or defending differences. Praying levels the playing field. We're all submitting to God's sovereignty, in the presence of His love, at the feet of His mercies. Prayer is the proving ground when we choose to love people regardless of opposing views, opinions, or beliefs.

How much time do we spend praying for others? We might be separated by a lot of things in a lot of ways, but prayer brings us together in heavenly places, as our whispers, voices, and even the silent pleas of our hearts are heard and held in high regard. James 5:16 (NIV) says, "Pray for each other so that you may be healed. The prayer of a righteous person is powerful and effective."

When we pray, we have the undivided attention of the almighty God, a privilege beyond our human comprehension. And when we speak the Word of God in prayer, we have the attention of angels who stand ready to act on those words. Psalm 103:20 NKJV says, "Bless the LORD, you His angels, who excel in strength, who do His Word, heeding the voice of His word." Praying is part of loving people—and loving people is second only to loving God.

Give me wisdom and compassion to pray for others, Lord, with love and without ceasing.

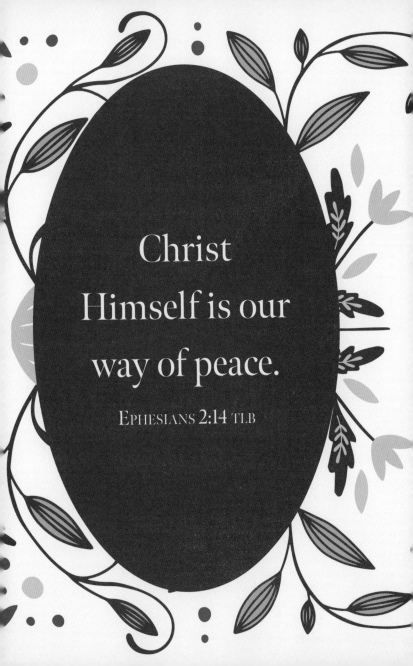

Christ Himself is our way of peace.

EPHESIANS 2:14 TLB

STRENGTH MADE PERFECT

God is strong, and He wants you strong.

EPHESIANS 6:10 THE MESSAGE

Staying strong when we feel incapable of doing so. . .in the midst of suffering and sorrow, when the unexpected hits and leaves us feeling helpless, in moments when our emotions swell and our courage cowers. . .that's where we learn God's strength is made perfect in our weakness. On the other side of the storm, we look back and see how He brought us through when our heart was breaking to the point of too many tears and too little hope, and we stand in awe of His faithfulness. . .again. We grow stronger with every "again," more confident of God's tender care, and more sure of His perfect love for us. It is unwavering.

God wants us strong because our source of strength is His power within us, and that's what He wants us to be immovably certain of. He wants us to declare, in every battle we face, "I can do all things through Christ who strengthens me" (Philippians 4:13 NKJV). A greater dependence on Him will always result in a greater faith in us. The two can't be separated. We live, move, and have our being in Him—and that makes us stronger than we ever thought possible.

Your strength is my overcoming power, Lord.
I trust Your love in every trial I meet.

BRIGHT AND BOLD

Because of this light within you,
you should do only what is good
and right and true.

EPHESIANS 5:9 TLB

The desire to do what is good, right, and true has nothing to do with who we are or what we want and everything to do with the light that entered our life when Jesus did. His light shines on what's important to God—and it illuminates every relationship in our lives. Life is designed to be done together. Love thrives in connecting with people, in doing what's good and right for others, and in putting truth in the spotlight: God is gentle, forgiving, merciful, and kind; God is compassionate, caring, attentive, and good; God is patient, thoughtful, generous, and wise.

Every characteristic of love is every bright and bold thing we should be. When a person believes they're loved deeply, wherever they are on their journey, the light of Christ exposes the darkness that causes them to believe otherwise. Division is an evil stronghold, and love is how we dismantle it. Today is another gift God has given us to do what love does. We're here for each other, for love's sake, and for God's glory. Nothing matters more than the people He puts in our lives. . . and nothing makes more of a difference than love.

Let the light within me draw others to You, Lord.

MATTERS OF
THE HEART

Don't be fools; be wise.

We can never take lightly our responsibility to do what God created us to do—love Him and love people. It would be foolish to deceive ourselves into thinking our words and actions are lightweight things, having no bearing on how the world sees God. "The wisdom that comes from heaven is first of all pure and full of quiet gentleness. Then it is peace-loving and courteous. It allows discussion and is willing to yield to others; it is full of mercy and good deeds. It is wholehearted and straightforward and sincere" (James 3:17 TLB). Divine wisdom delivers a weighty blow to anything unlike the love of God. Wisdom respects love. It's honest about grace, the freely given favor of our fully forgiving God. Wisdom from heaven puts love first, keeping our differences at bay.

God doesn't expect us to defend His unconditional love by sounding cymbals and elevating arguments.

Wisdom teaches us to be full of quiet gentleness, peace, and courtesy. Love will do its eternal work in the hearts of others by way of love's qualities: patience, kindness, humility, selflessness, and forgiveness. God asks us to put those qualities on display in our lives and allow Him to handle the matters of the heart.

*Make me a straightforward
and shining example of Your love, Lord.
Give me wisdom to be wholeheartedly invested
in loving people the way You do.*

LOVE WITHOUT FEAR

Be careful how you act; these are difficult days.

EPHESIANS 5:15 TLB

These are difficult days. The suffering and trials on a worldwide scope compel us to pray without stopping. And they might, if we're not careful, tempt us to change the course of what God has called us to do. It feels comforting to stay in when we should be reaching out. Fear is at a fever pitch. Still—there's no room to doubt God's control or think for a moment we're not in His care. Our trust is secure in Him, and love is the way we'll see each other through.

This is the time to encourage one another by being present, listening long, and giving generously. We are to "bear one another's burdens, and so fulfill the law of Christ" (Galatians 6:2 NKJV). The things that we see will never alter the plan of God that we can't fully know, for "the plans of the LORD stand firm forever, the purposes of His heart through all generations" (Psalm 33:11 NIV). We need to hold tightly to one another and love wholeheartedly every day. In confident faith we need to live fearlessly and believe God is our shield, our refuge, and our strength. Loving people well holds a higher purpose than anything else we do. . .because it offers God the highest praise we can give.

I ask for courage to open my heart
and my hand to do Your will, Lord.

WITH EVERY BREATH

Sing praises over everything,
any excuse for a song to God the Father.

❧ EPHESIANS 5:20 The Message ❧

After all God has done, praise and thanksgiving should flow from us like a river that has no chance of drying up. Yet we're all guilty of shifting our focus to all that's wrong in our relationships, our lives, and the world. It's an ongoing battle between our spirit and our flesh—one that won't be completely settled until our earthly journey has ended. Until then we need to practice and prioritize praise.

To begin your days on a high note, why not start with a song that steals your attention from your to-do list to the truth that God is our everything—our hope, our high tower, our help, and our healer? Not one thing that comes against us is higher than He is. The name of Jesus is set above everything. He promised us an abundant life, and the blood He shed seals our victory. If we spend our days singing, praying, hoping, and loving, we win back our lives moment by moment. Distractions and disappointments will come, but we can restart the rejoicing with every next breath we're given. God is good all the time. . .and all the time we have can be used to exalt Him.

I praise You for who You are and everything You are to me, Lord. Your goodness and love follow me all the days of my life.

TELLING AND HEARING

Talk with each other much about the Lord.

➤• EPHESIANS 5:19 TLB •◄

What builds our spiritual muscles more than getting together to talk about God and what He's done in our lives? Every time we brag on God's goodness, it magnifies His greatness and makes us brave. Telling and hearing God-glorifying testimonies fills us with courage. It increases our joy. It reveals the multitude of ways God can and will work in our circumstances to bring about what is best for us. We learn that even when it's dark and we can't see the way out or through, God has a plan in place to part the sea for our safe passage. We can trust Him.

There's something special about being together in the presence of God to collectively call out His faithfulness. Jesus said, "Where two or three gather together because they are Mine, I will be right there among them" (Matthew 18:20 TLB). It feels good to be

His, and it's encouraging to be together. It confirms the truth that He wants us to hold on to each other through life, with all of its hard days and wilderness stretches. God can be called upon and counted on, no matter how many times we stumble and fall. His grace never depends on our good behavior—it rests solely on His unfailing love.

I know togetherness is the desire of Your heart, Lord.
Use me to encourage others as we serve You.

REFLECTING JOY

*Give thanks for everything to our God and Father
in the name of our Lord Jesus Christ.*

EPHESIANS 5:20 TLB

Giving thanks translates. When we have a thankful heart, our words, actions, and faces express joy. Not the joy that comes from things going right outwardly, but from things being right inwardly. That's where true joy manifests. When our hearts and minds join forces to thank God for all He is and what we have in Jesus, our countenance reflects it, and people see it.

Joy is one of those infectious qualities that can shed light in darkness, change the energy in a room from negative to positive, and bring smiles where frowns once were. It's one of the best supernatural powers God gives us! People are more receptive to the love God gives through us when His joy is alive within us. The surest way to keep joy activated is to keep being thankful in every season of our lives.

When the valley is lower than we think we can go and the climb is longer than we think we can manage, thank God for the mountaintop view we know is coming. He said, "Fear not, for I am with you. Do not be dismayed. I am your God. I will strengthen you; I will help you; I will uphold you with My victorious right hand" (Isaiah 41:10 TLB).

I thank You for taking care of everything that concerns me, Lord. You are my hope and joy.

YOUR PRICELESS PLACE

Christ's love makes the church whole.
His words evoke her beauty.

❧ EPHESIANS 5:26 THE MESSAGE ❧

We're part of a beautiful whole. Each of us is an irreplaceable thread in the fabric of God's perfect design. The unique gifts you have are needed, no matter what you've been told or how this world makes you feel. The way Jesus sees you is the true you, completely wrapped in love and complete in Him alone. There is no people-pleasing necessary to prove your worth or your special place in His plan.

God's Word brings out the beauty in you, reveals the priceless gift you are, and speaks of the infinite value He puts on your life:

"You are precious and honored in My sight"
(Isaiah 43:4 NIV).

"[You are] fearfully and wonderfully made"
(Psalm 139:14 NKJV).

"I know the plans I have for you, says the Lord. They are plans for good and not for evil, to give you a future and a hope" (Jeremiah 29:11 TLB).

"Be sure of this—that I am with you always, even to the end of the world" (Matthew 28:20 TLB).

Standing in the confidence of God's Word, we can go fearlessly into our days and boldly into our purpose—and that will always include helping others see themselves the way God sees them.

Your Word is the truth that guides me, Lord.
In You I find my worth and purpose.

LOVE IN MOTION

He has no favorites.

EPHESIANS 6:9 TLB

In a world of social media influencers, a world in which significance is often measured by emojis indicating like, love, care, and laughter, it's good to remember that God has no favorites. Not one of us is more important than another to Him—and His love matters most. God's love is unconditional, kind, compassionate, and everlasting. It reaches to the depths of our failures and shortcomings to pull us into the light of forgiveness and grace. In Jesus we stand equal to one another with a clean slate and a price tag that reads "invaluable."

Falling prey to the temptation to think that, because we have more followers or millions of views, we're more important than any other person for whom Jesus died is a dangerous trap. It can become a distraction that's hard to control. God wants us to look up. He wants us to spend time together undistracted by our phones and invested in loving and encouraging each other. Life is hard, and we need our human support system. It's meant to be part of God's constant care and active involvement in our trials. A simple hug, a word of truth, or talking with someone about how God carried us through what they're going through are things we can't afford to bypass. God loves others through our willingness to let Him. . .and His love is always in motion.

*Let me be a vessel of Your love and care
for every person, Lord.*

THE GOOD PATH

Don't act thoughtlessly,
but try to find out and do whatever
the Lord wants you to.

EPHESIANS 5:17 TLB

G uarding our thoughts and our hearts is a wise way forward if we want to fulfill God's commandments to love Him and the people He created. Racing through our days one rushed routine after another can lead to missing opportunities to slow down enough to do that. God understands the pressures of this life at a time like this. Nothing is a surprise to Him. The world is vastly different, and the demands on us are much greater than they used to be. It's up to us to ask for help.

Psalm 139:10 (TLB) says, "Your hand will guide me, Your strength will support me." One thing that hasn't changed is the fact that God is here with the same amazing grace and the same unfailing love. We can pray, "O Lord, the earth is full of Your loving-kindness! Teach me Your good paths" (Psalm 119:64

TLB). When we ask, God answers. We tend to tangle things up and make them harder than they need to be. If we pray for God to lead us, we need simply to trust the steps we're taking. Our hearts will tell us which way to go because the Holy Spirit will help us know. If we're thoughtful, prayerful, and humble, God will faithfully guide.

I want to walk in the center of Your will, Lord.
Show me the way.

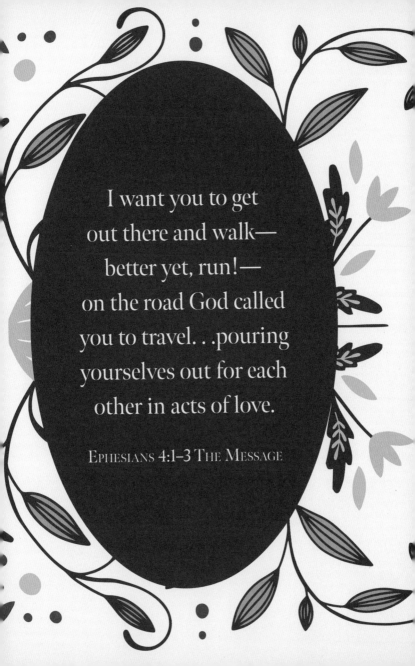

I want you to get
out there and walk—
better yet, run!—
on the road God called
you to travel. . .pouring
yourselves out for each
other in acts of love.

EPHESIANS 4:1–3 THE MESSAGE

CHOSEN BY LOVE

Work with a smile on your face,
always keeping in mind that no matter
who happens to be giving the orders,
you're really serving God.

❧· EPHESIANS 6:7 The Message ·❧

Unlike our worldly work schedules, serving God is a twenty-four-hour privilege that comes with eternal rewards. It's not always easy to keep that in mind when people and differing personalities challenge our joyful attitudes in the workplace. It is, however, a deeply satisfying truth to get into the habit of acting upon. When we trust that God puts us in jobs, places, and people's lives for a good reason, we're better able to manage our thoughts and emotions when it feels like we're working in an environment that is less than wonderful.

With a constant mindset and confidence that God is orchestrating every part of our lives with perfect timing, we can know we're right where we need to be—either for ourselves or for the people around us. There's a very good chance it's a bit of both. "He chose us in Him before the creation of the world" (Ephesians 1:4 NIV). Being sure God knew the story of our lives before time began is not only reassuring, it's one of the best ways to transform our thinking and work with a smile on our face—knowing every page of our stories was written with love.

Serving You brings me joy, Lord.
I'm thankful that all of my days
are designed with love.

STANDING READY

God's Word is an indispensable weapon.

EPHESIANS 6:16 The Message

There are many things we can live without, but if we want an abundant, fulfilling life, God's Word isn't one of them. God's Word is the lifeline to God's power. It's the weapon we have at our disposal every minute of every day to use against every lie that enters our minds.

Ephesians 6:14 (NKJV) says, "Stand therefore, having girded your waist with truth." In Roman times, a soldier's belt served as the foundational piece of his entire suit of armor, holding his sword in place, supporting him in battle, and binding the rest of his armor together. It can't be any clearer. To know and use God's Word is to secure our victory—fear loses, anxiety surrenders, condemnation is crushed, and hope soars. The lies launched against us seek to make us feel doubtful, discouraged, and defeated, but they have no chance of succeeding when we're armed with the Word of God: "For the weapons of our warfare are not carnal but mighty in God for pulling down strongholds, casting down arguments and every high thing that exalts itself against the knowledge of God, bringing every thought into captivity to the obedience of Christ" (II Corinthians 10:4-5 NKJV). When we capture and replace every lie with truth, we start to win where the battle begins.

Fill my thoughts with truth, Lord.

OUR PEOPLE

Whatever good anyone does,
he will receive the same from the Lord.

>・ EPHESIANS 6:8 NKJV ・<

When God promises a harvest of good for the good things we do, we can get excited about what's coming. Doing good involves helping one another through life. It reveals the heart of God for us when we turn to each other for friendship, encouragement, and support. Leaning on the people in our lives does nothing to indicate individual weakness and everything to prove God's faithfulness and goodness. We are His hands and feet in this world.

Seclusion sets us up for defeat, but when we surround ourselves with friends and serve one another in love, we're strengthened. Even when we least feel like being part of a community or we think we have nothing left to give at the end of a long day, that might be the time we need togetherness the most. God knit us together with the need to be together. The early church understood this inherent need, a desire God put in each of us. Acts 2:44 (TLB) tells us, "All the believers met together constantly and shared everything with each other." The joy God gives multiplies when we give to each other. Whether it be material, emotional, or spiritual needs, God connects us to the people who best meet them for the purpose of building our faith in Him.

I praise You for the people in my life, Lord.
They are good gifts.

OUR WINDOW IN TIME

Keep your eyes open.
Keep each other's spirits up so that
no one falls behind or drops out.

EPHESIANS 6:18 THE MESSAGE

We sometimes don't realize the power God puts in each of us to do His wonderful work in this world. We take for granted the gifts we've been given, the marvelous way we've been created, and the magnitude of what He's equipped us to accomplish in the lives of others. We're chosen to be on this earth for this specific window in time. We have much to do!

Every day brings a sunrise filled with mercy, leaving no excuse of past mistakes to hold us back. Every whisper from the Holy Spirit presents another chance to do the things God planned for us to do, so we have opportunities to do good every day. The smallest kindnesses—opening doors; yielding in traffic; offering a smile, a thank-you, or a sincere, "How are you doing?"—can be a seed for God to cultivate. Love isn't a complicated thing; it's an eternal gift planted in a simple act of good. We are the doers of God's goodness. We should go through our days in prayerful willingness with our hearts open wide. A surrendered heart and an open hand can deliver little miracles from a faithful God. . .and make the landscape of our lives more beautiful than we imagined.

Show me how to love others with Your heart, Lord, sowing good seeds wherever I go.

SUITING UP

*Put on all of God's armor so that
you will be able to stand safe against
all strategies and tricks of Satan.*

EPHESIANS 6:11 TLB

There's a strategist at work in our lives who wants nothing more than to trip us up and defy our God-given purpose. Thankfully, God equips us with everything we need to scramble and scrub the enemy's efforts. We're safe in the armor God supplies—truth, righteousness, readiness, faith, and salvation—with a banner over us that reads "Jesus." We need nothing more to live the life God gives through the promises He's made. If we hope to faithfully follow the commandments to love Him and love people, then isn't it possible that it's time to suit up? Isn't it possible that we need to be there for each other? In fact, it's much easier to put on a suit of armor with the help of another person.

In the difficult things we face and the trials we go through, our confidence and resolve are strength-

ened by companionship. There's comfort in knowing we're not alone, and there's joy in being there for
someone else. It's a divinely ordered design, and it
makes God rejoice to see it. Love is never a one-sid-
ed, selfish, or solitary thing; it's an openly generous
and selfless gift, meant to be passed between us in a
continual exchange.

You've given me the win, Lord,
no matter what I face.
Give me strength to suit up for today
and follow Your lead with love.

RAISING THE SHIELD

Take up the shield of faith,
with which you can extinguish
all the flaming arrows of the evil one.

EPHESIANS 6:16 NIV

If we can visualize a barrage of flaming arrows coming toward us every day, we can be more diligent about holding our shield of faith up and in front of us. "Faith is confidence in what we hope for and assurance about what we do not see" (Hebrews 11:1 NIV). We hope to see God's power in our lives. We hope to do His perfect will. We hope to love our neighbors, live with humility, and learn to walk in faith with more certainty every day. And we hope to please God with every breath we take. It's a process of discovering how unconditionally and infinitely we're loved, with a love we can't lose or destroy by any mistake we make, any number of times we walk away, or any amount of shame in which we feel stuck.

The shield of faith quenches the fire on any

flaming arrow headed our way and awakens every attribute of God's eternal love. Our heavenly Father said, "I have loved you with an everlasting love. . .with lovingkindness I have drawn you" (Jeremiah 31:3 NKJV). We are drawn to His side by love and lifted to certain victory by faith—a faith that creates a shield against anything that attempts to destroy us with doubt.

I know that without faith
it's impossible to please You, Lord.
Let Your love consume every doubt
I have today.

KEEPING THE CONVERSATION OPEN

Prayer is essential in this ongoing warfare.

❧ EPHESIANS 6:16 THE MESSAGE ❧

Prayer is our place of perfect peace. It's having the undivided attention of the best Listener, the truest Friend, the kindest Father, and the purest Love. God is everything our hearts were created to crave and every desire we yearn to fulfill. Even on our darkest days, our hope is anchored deeply in the power of prayer. Going through our days with an open flow of conversation with the Father is going to get us through with a peace of mind the world can't give. Staying connected spiritually enables us to make a profound difference physically. We're more likely to live fearlessly and love people fully. We're better able to forgive quickly and move forward freely. We're grounded in our faith, sure of our purpose, and hopeful in spite of what we see.

When our prayer lives are healthy, our earthly lives are as they should be—dependent on God, abundant in Christ, and guided by the Holy Spirit. Actively praying keeps us outright loving and tirelessly thankful, which fills our hearts with God's favorite things.

Create in me a pure and prayerful heart, Lord.
Let Your perfect love fill my life with peace.

LOVE'S FOCUS

Long before He laid down earth's foundations,
He had us in mind, had settled on us
as the focus of His love,
to be made whole and holy by His love.

EPHESIANS 1:4 THE MESSAGE

God had us on His mind before time began and held us securely in His love for the lives we now live. With our first breath, the journey began, and the battle ensued. Life is at once a beautiful gift and a perilous love story. As we face constant thoughts that we are undeserving of God's love and forgiveness, the Holy Spirit is at work assuring us of the finished work of the cross: "God brought you alive—right along with Christ! Think of it! All sins forgiven, the slate wiped clean" (Colossians 2:15 THE MESSAGE).

We've been the focus of God's love before He laid the foundations of the earth, and His focus hasn't shifted. You are in the center of His thoughts. Your life is under His loving and watchful eye. In Him your future is filled with hope and purpose. Nothing can move His gaze, and nothing can stop His plan for your one amazing, irreplaceable life. On any of your days, there's one truth to lift high and hold on to: God loved you so much that He gave His Son, His one and only Son, to give you whole and everlasting life (see John 3:16).

Thank You for loving me to life, Lord.
My heart rejoices in You.

EVERYDAY STRENGTH

*Oh, the utter extravagance
of His work in us who trust Him—
endless energy, boundless strength!*

EPHESIANS 1:19 The Message

The pressures of life can push us far away from the things we need most. Our energy is often spent before we can think about doing things to cultivate togetherness and strengthen our relationships. Thankfully, God's work in us is never sluggish or slowed down by time constraints and too many things to do. Trusting Him every day to give us the strength we need, emotionally and physically, gives us the energy to follow through with what He asks us to do.

Often the easiest things to push aside end up being the really important things we need—and only God can know that. The priceless times spent with family and friends are among them, as are the avenues of giving God has encouraged us to take that we haven't yet stepped into. It's easy to justify putting things aside if we don't depend on Him for boldness, courage, strength, and determination, because we can't do them alone. Jesus said, "I am the vine; you are the branches. If you remain in Me and I in you, you will bear much fruit; apart from Me you can do nothing" (John 15:5 NIV). The things that matter most in life happen when we depend on Him most to accomplish them.

*Strengthen me to bear the fruit that
leads others to You, Lord.*

THE FUTURE
HE HOLDS

God can do anything, you know—
far more than you could ever imagine
or guess or request in your wildest dreams!
He does it not by pushing us around
but by working within us, His Spirit
deeply and gently within us.

EPHESIANS 3:20-21 THE MESSAGE

When it comes to living out the priceless purpose of our lives, we can be absolutely sure of this: God is never rude, Jesus is never unkind, and the Holy Spirit is never pushy. We can't imagine the scope of goodness God wants to pour into our lives, and He's fully able to make it happen whenever He chooses. In His infinite wisdom it will come at the perfectly appointed time and as a direct result of His Spirit working deeply within us.

Our lives are a daily preparation for the future God holds. In His kind and gentle way, He transforms our hearts with love in order for us to be His love in this world. What we get in this material world will fall into the shadows of what we give to affect eternity—and with that realization will come a joy we never thought possible. The more we mature into the practice of loving God by loving people, the more fulfilling our lives will be. . .and the more amazed we'll be at the miracles in store.

I surrender to the loving and gentle shaping
of my heart in Your hands, Lord.
Let my life bring You glory.

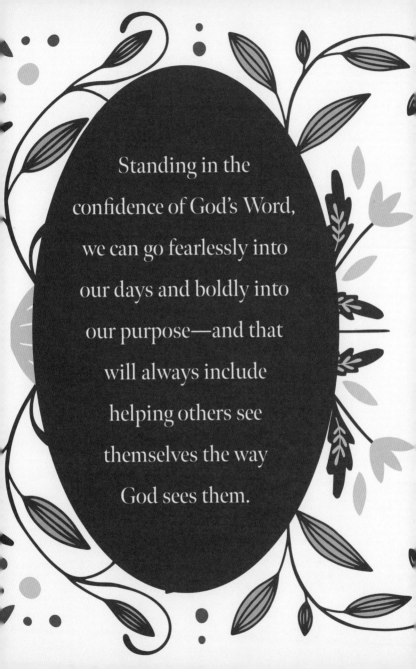

Standing in the confidence of God's Word, we can go fearlessly into our days and boldly into our purpose—and that will always include helping others see themselves the way God sees them.

A FORMIDABLE FORCE

*You were all called to travel on the same road
and in the same direction, so stay together,
both outwardly and inwardly.*

>. **EPHESIANS 4:4 THE MESSAGE** .<

We have unique gifts, diverse paths, individual challenges, and different places we call home. Together, we have a single purpose in the service of a wonderful Savior—to stay together beneath the umbrella of love. "Try always to be led along together by the Holy Spirit and so be at peace with one another" (Ephesians 4:3 TLB).

God sent the Holy Spirit to be our Friend, the One brought alongside us to help in our time of need. Separately, God knew we could accomplish little to fill the world with His love, but acting as one body with one mind for the purpose of magnifying unity and grace, we become a formidable force for good. We are not to follow the pattern of this world that emphasizes divisiveness—love's way of doing things is sticking together, being there for one another, and gathering together to encourage each other in our faith. Jesus prayed a perfect prayer for us: "My prayer for all of them is that they will be of one heart and mind, just as You and I are, Father—that just as You are in Me and I am in You, so they will be in Us, and the world will believe You sent Me" (John 17:21 TLB).

Let the love I show others lead them to You, Lord.

THE GROWING NEED

Speaking the truth in love,
we will grow to become in every respect
the mature body of Him who is the head,
that is, Christ.

❧ EPHESIANS 4:15 NIV ☙

Love grows where Christ shows. He can be seen in the way we treat people, the patience we exercise in a crowded grocery store, the kindness in the way we speak to the wait staff, and the compassion we express to those having a tough time in this world. When we slow down and open our eyes to take in a wider view of what's going on around us, we'll see the growing need for truth and love.

Our daily routines can cause us to have a narrow vision of the needs in this world. Maybe it's time to take a look at every aspect of our lives in Jesus—the way we speak, the way we react, the time we make for others, and the importance we put on being together. We have enough to do, our lists are long, and our time is already stretched to its limit. But love is God's heart, and people are priceless in His eyes. If He can't love them through us, we aren't loving Him in truth. Today is a good day to take every chance we have to be every good thing He is.

Make me a humble servant of Your love, Lord.
Reveal the needs around me.

GLORIOUS UNITY

The whole body, joined and held together
by every supporting ligament,
grows and builds itself up in love,
as each part does its work.

❧• EPHESIANS 4:16 NIV •❦

Are we doing the work of unity? Are we using the wisdom we've gained to encourage others, practicing the characteristics of love and offering forgiveness freely and quickly? Each of us is an irreplaceable part of a beautiful whole. What makes our togetherness so beautiful is the reflection of Jesus it creates. He said, "I have given them the glory You gave Me—the glorious unity of being one, as We are—I in them and You in Me, all being perfected into one—so that the world will know You sent Me and will understand that You love them as much as You love Me" (John 17:22-23 TLB).

Unity brings a twofold blessing. Being in harmony makes each of us feel valued and brings glory to the Father—and that glory draws the world to His love for them. He loves every human He created as much as He loves His only Son. That truth is expressed by our understanding that we are one with Him. . .and by our willingness to work as a unified expression of His amazing love.

Help me work together and do my part, Lord,
and glorify God through oneness with You.

SPOTLIGHT ON LOVE

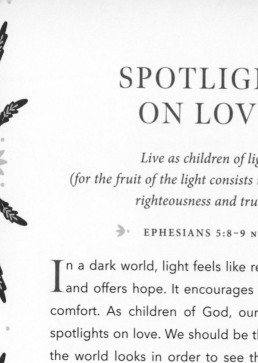

Live as children of light
(for the fruit of the light consists in all goodness,
righteousness and truth).

EPHESIANS 5:8–9 NIV

In a dark world, light feels like relief. It calms fear and offers hope. It encourages good and brings comfort. As children of God, our lives should be spotlights on love. We should be the ones to whom the world looks in order to see the way, the truth, and the life that Jesus is (see John 14:6). Being one with Him means the purpose of our light is to expose God's love in full. His love lets everyone know they're valuable, no matter what their social status is; it lets every individual know they're seen, no matter how they've been abused and neglected; it lets every person on this earth know they're loved without condition, no matter how undeserving they feel.

This is the time to let the light of Jesus pierce through the sin-stained pain that people are going through to reveal the grace-filled peace they need. God's love can soothe every heartache, heal every wound, and remove every shard of shame. Love is our singular hope for a brighter world—and God has called us to put it in plain sight.

Let my life be a testimony of Your love on full display, Lord.

A SECURE HOPE

Give thanks for everything to God the Father.

EPHESIANS 5:20 NLT

The discipline of being thankful at all times and in every season of life is an important one. A grateful attitude gains us a joyful outlook, and joy is vital too. "The joy of the Lord is your strength" (Nehemiah 8:10 TLB). There can be no true joy in our lives without a deep-seated trust in God.

As humans, we'd certainly like to be in control of the timing of answered prayers, the level of suffering we endure, and the ordering of every step we take. But we'd soon discover what a mess we'd make. God loves us more than anyone else can, and He knows us better than anyone else will. Nothing in this life should make us more thankful than knowing His love is leading the way. It should quench our worry and calm our anxiety. It should smother every thought that tries to tell us God isn't working every single thing together for our good—even when the road to get there is long. Giving thanks for everything to

God, our unfailing Father, secures our hope in His love and keeps us steadily strengthened for our journey. He's our Refuge and Redeemer. . .and our grateful heart proves it.

You're my security, my strength, and my hope, Lord. My life is safe in Your love.

BEAUTIFUL YOU

*Out of the generosity of Christ,
each of us is given his own gift.*

EPHESIANS 4:8 The Message

You are unique. You're fearfully and wonderfully made, with a different set of traits than anyone else and a specific collection of gifts to use for God's glory. No one else in the whole wide world is exactly like you. When God looks at you, He sees your one-of-a-kind beauty—and He'll spend your entire earthbound journey helping you see it too.

When you see yourself the way God sees you, your love-redeemed soul shines brighter. The world looks at you and sees not only your beauty, but His. Your life becomes a God-glorifying expression of the love that restores light to dimly lit places and redeems lives that are shattered. When God gives, He gives generously. The gifts you've been given are many, and the love by which they came is deeper than we can know. Trust Him with everything that concerns you and live each day with the confidence of knowing there's nothing you can do to make Him turn His back on you. You're at the center of His thoughts, in the palm of His hand, and in the direct, unswerving path of His incredible, unstoppable love.

Thank You for Your marvelous work in me, Lord.
Your love is everything I need.

ALL WE NEED

I insist—and God backs me up on this—
that there be no going along with the crowd,
the empty-headed, mindless crowd.

>• EPHESIANS 4:17 THE MESSAGE •<

Blending in with those around us makes our lives lackluster. The light and love of God becomes overshadowed by complacency and being comfortable with mediocrity. Living with humility and conviction doesn't mean separating ourselves from the lost, but being among them the way Jesus was—with an unmistakable light and the Father's unconditional love. The light shone into their darkness and drew them to the One who loved them with His whole heart, to the point of giving His life to prove it. We are now the bearers of that light and the carriers of His love to the people He brings into our lives and across our paths.

It isn't coincidence when our hearts are moved to help someone, call a friend, visit a neighbor, or give to meet a need. God's love is moving in us constantly.

The Holy Spirit is filling us with truth faithfully. The grace of Jesus is guiding our spirits peacefully and sufficiently. He's given us all we need to do all we can for the good of everyone we meet.

Use my life for the undeniable light of Your glory, Lord. Let me be a pillar of Your love in this world.

CONNECTED BY LOVE

In Christ's body we're all connected to each other.

EPHESIANS 4:25 The Message

When there's division and disconnect in the body of Christ, it's up to us to get closer to Him. He's the healing balm, the healthy perspective, and the perfect counsel. When we get too involved in solving problems and deciding which way is the right way to create unity, we miss the mark. It is never about us, how we feel, or how wise our opinion sounds. Jesus is our perfect pattern, and love is our perfect rule of conduct.

"If I speak in the tongues of men or of angels, but do not have love, I am only a resounding gong or a clanging cymbal. If I have the gift of prophecy and can fathom all mysteries and all knowledge, and if I have a faith that can move mountains, but do not have love, I am nothing. If I give all I possess to the poor and give over my body to hardship that I may boast, but do not have love, I gain nothing"

(I Corinthians 13:1–3 NIV). These words of truth should be our read-aloud to start every day. We are connected by love, and connecting with people and nurturing our relationships is God's plan for our lives. Love is fulfilling on every level, and being sure of that will bring only His best.

I surrender my thoughts
and actions to You today, Lord.
Fill me with Your love and wisdom.

GOD SENDS GIFTS

Say only what helps, each word a gift.

EPHESIANS 4:29 THE MESSAGE

E motions can flare, and the wrong words can fly when we feel stressed, stretched too thin, and under a mountain of pressure. That's not an unusual set of circumstances in a world that's moving faster than ever. Thank God we have each other. When one of us is anxious, God sends the friend who's calming. When we feel helpless in a sea of situations that are out of our control, God puts people in place to say, "I'm praying for you, and God is carrying you. We're going to get through this together."

The compassion of God cannot and will not fail. Just as the right words are gifts, so are the people who speak them. Every good and perfect gift comes to us from God, and not only is He the best gift giver, He knows exactly when to send them to us. He never needs a special occasion—you being a priceless gift to Him is more than enough. He wraps every good thing He gives in His perfect love and binds it with all the grace you need to live an abundantly blessed life. Take a deep breath today as you whisper a heartfelt thank-You for all He's done. It will reset the stress you feel to the calm you need—and inspire your words and actions to be gifts of His infinite love.

Thank You for knowing me so well and sending just what I need, Lord. My heart is full.

EMBRACED BY LOVE

Immense in mercy
and with an incredible love,
He embraced us.

EPHESIANS 2:5 THE MESSAGE

God gives hugs. He gives them through our people. He gives them in gorgeous sunrises and starlit nights. He gives them in unexpected kindnesses and unearned grace. God's goodness toward us has no off switch. We're the object of His love and the joy of His heart. Zephaniah 3:18 (TLB) says, "Is that a joyous choir I hear? No, it is the Lord Himself exulting over you in happy song."

Whenever we have doubtful days, and we'll certainly have them, our way back to confident faith is watching with expectation for the hugs God will send—and when they come, we need to embrace Him back with gratefulness and praise. He's our Comforter at all times. . .when our days are long and hard, when we feel underappreciated and overworked, when we push through the difficult hours in quiet prayer. We're in His thoughts no matter how we feel, and believing that truth in spite of our feelings can bring us a comfort we never thought possible. We can praise God, saying, "You are my hiding place from every storm of life" (Psalm 32:7 TLB). God is for us—as our shield, our strength, our hope, and our victory—and in our Father's arms, we are hugged, held, and loved.

All my days are in Your hands, Lord.
Let me live each one leaning on You.

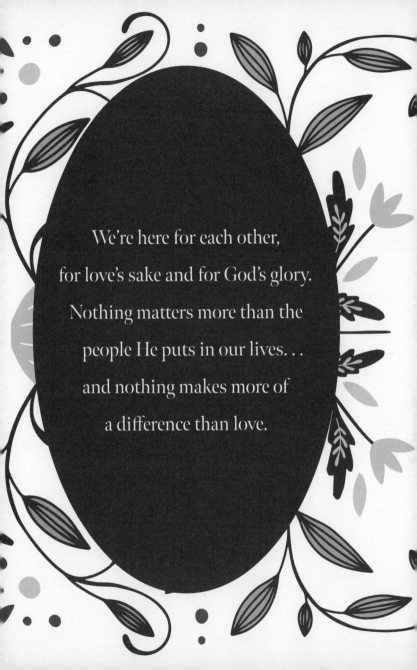

We're here for each other,
for love's sake and for God's glory.
Nothing matters more than the
people He puts in our lives. . .
and nothing makes more of
a difference than love.

LIVE YOUR FAITH

Dear Friend,

This book was prayerfully crafted with you, the reader, in mind. Every word, every sentence, every page was thoughtfully written, designed, and packaged to encourage you—right where you are this very moment. At DaySpring, our vision is to see every person experience the life-changing message of God's love. So, as we worked through rough drafts, design changes, edits, and details, we prayed for you to deeply experience His unfailing love, indescribable peace, and pure joy. It is our sincere hope that through these Truth-filled pages your heart will be blessed, knowing that God cares about you—your desires and disappointments, your challenges and dreams.

He knows. He cares. He loves you unconditionally.

BLESSINGS!
THE DAYSPRING BOOK TEAM

Additional copies of this book and
other DaySpring titles can be purchased
at fine retailers everywhere.
Order online at <u>dayspring.com</u>
or
by phone at 1-877-751-4347

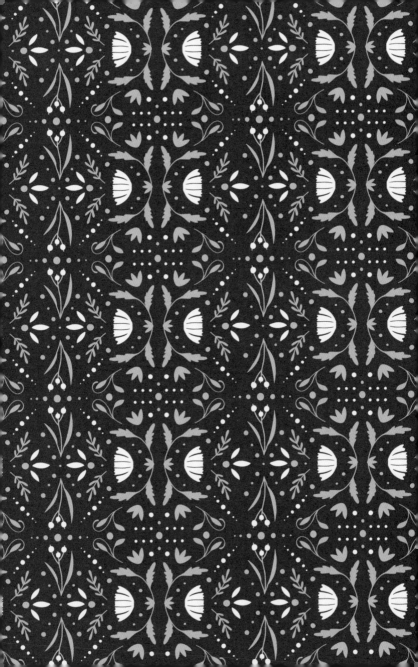